Look at Me When I Talk to You

EAL Learners in Non-EAL Classrooms

SYLVIA HELMER
CATHERINE EDDY

Pippin

Designed by John Zehethofer
Typeset by Gwen Peroni
Printed and bound in Canada by Friesens

Library and Archives Canada Cataloguing in Publication

Helmer, Sylvia, 1948-
Look at me when I talk to you : EAL learners
in non-EAL classrooms / Sylvia Helmer,
Catherine L. Eddy. – 3rd ed.

(Pippin teacher's library ; 47)
Includes bibliographical references.
ISBN 978-0-88751-122-6

    1. English language—Study and teaching as a second language.
2. Minorities—Education. 3. Communication in education.
I. Eddy, Catherine L., 1947- II. Title. III. Series: Pippin teacher's
library ; 47

PE1128.A2H453 2012   428.0071'5   C2012-901725-6

10 9 8 7 6 5 4 3 2 1

This book is dedicated to the many EAL learners in whose presence we have had the opportunity to teach—and to learn.

In addition, this book owes much to friends and colleagues, who have listened, read, critiqued and provided insights, anecdotes and reflections. We are grateful also to family and loved ones who have supported our efforts.

Responsibility for the content is, of course, ours.

. . . .

CONTENTS

. . . .

INTRODUCTION

People don't get along
because they fear each other.
People fear each other
because they don't know each other.
They don't know each other
because they have not properly communicated with each
other.

Martin Luther King, Jr.

Culture is complex. Communication is complex. And working with students from a variety of ethnic and cultural backgrounds provides ample evidence that this complexity is greater than the sum of its parts.

This book is intended for teachers of all grade levels who instruct students whose home language is not English and whose cultural backgrounds vary. Over time, various terms have come in and out of fashion—English as a second language (ESL), English as an additional language (EAL), limited English proficient (LEP) and English-language learners (ELLs). The term EAL learner will be used throughout this book as we feel it celebrates an asset and an accomplishment that these learners are bringing, namely at least one intact language, and that they are now learning an additional language.

Though many books deal with aspects of culture or communication, this book combines these elements by describing and interpreting potential scenarios experienced by classroom teachers.

Whenever teachers work with EAL learners, gaps in communication will arise for a variety of reasons. First, a simple lack of English skills creates the potential for miscommunication. In addition, there are significant differences in the way individuals habitually interact with others, especially when they are from different cultural or ethnic backgrounds.

When these differences are associated with additional language learners in any classroom, they can create communication breakdowns that go beyond simply a lack of linguistic ability in English. There has been a tendency to consider both language learning and these less tangible ways of interacting and "being" to be the sole responsibility of the language support specialist. A typical reaction is: "I'm not a language teacher; I teach math (or music, or science, etc.). Teaching English is the job of the EAL specialist."

But teaching EAL learners cannot and should not be the exclusive domain of the specialist. Because research in second-language acquisition clearly indicates that it takes five or more years to become fluent and proficient in a second language, responsibility for meeting the educational needs of these learners must realistically extend to all the teachers our EAL learners encounter.

In other words, we believe that working with and supporting students who are learning English as an additional language is the province of all teachers, no matter what their specialty. We will provide examples of differences in culture and communication throughout this book. The focus of this identification is to raise awareness and generate questions that will help all teachers consider alternative ways of thinking about how these differences may affect the teaching and learning that happen in their classrooms.

To sum up, this book has a dual purpose. It demonstrates that communication is so much more than simply the words spoken or written, and it provides some understandings about how to work optimally with EAL learners in any teaching and learning context. In writing the book, we hope to:

— Assist classroom teachers in their efforts to work with EAL learners in their classes.
— Raise awareness of both cultural differences and similarities, and how these may manifest themselves in everyday schooling situations.

— Increase empathy for and understanding of these similarities and differences.
— Pose questions for further exploration.

To this end, each chapter explores a different aspect of culture and communication, and each concludes with the opportunity for you to reflect on the content and to extend your thinking.

The first chapter, *Setting the Stage*, establishes the context by describing the changes that have occurred in our classrooms, schools and communities. It also addresses the concept of culture and the reasons we should consider its impact on communication, specifically in the classroom context.

Though the second chapter, *Awareness of Culture*, is an invitation to look at culture from several points of view, it focuses on encouraging us to think about the unique characteristics of our own culture, since any examination of culture must begin with the self. Having a greater understanding about how we conceptualize our own worldview will help us to understand how others might view that same world through different lenses.

The third chapter, *EAL Learners Are Individuals*, begins to address the question of who they are. "They" includes all those whose first or home language is not English, and who may originally be from anywhere around the globe.

The following chapter, *EAL Learners and Communication*, deals with aspects of communication across cultures, with particular emphasis on nonverbal communication. These cultural differences greatly influence our understanding of communication in general. Often-unexamined aspects of communication, such as gesture, tonal emphasis, touching, eye contact and personal space, are introduced and discussed.

Issues related to schooling are dealt with in Chapter Five, *EAL Learners and Schooling*. These include discussions of how to "do school" from suggested instructional strategies and techniques for dealing with a multicultural group, to defusing clashes between students from different cultural and linguistic backgrounds.

Having examined the more concrete elements of schooling, it is now important to consider that EAL learners are coming to our classrooms with increasingly diverse needs. There was a time when new immigrant groups arrived from a small number of areas of the world bringing with them very consistent patterns of background experiences. But those patterns of background experiences are no longer the case. Learners are arriving in our classrooms and schools from more and more areas around the globe. They are arriving with needs that go far beyond learning the English language in order to "do school" and successfully process the cultural adjustments that are entailed in enabling them to live and learn in a new land. Some special EAL learners, often those with additional learning needs, are the focus of Chapter Six, *Learning and Literacy for "Special" EAL Learners*.

Values and Beliefs is the focus of Chapter Seven. Underlying all aspects of culture and communication are basic beliefs about how the universe unfolds and how individuals should act and interact, even how parts of the body should be held, oriented and moved in given contexts. An appreciation and understanding of the way values and beliefs can mandate what happens in given communication contexts greatly enhances our ability to work with learners from many cultures.

The final chapter, *Putting It All Together*, provides practical applications for the ideas, strategies and techniques introduced in the preceding chapters. Questions frequently asked by classroom teachers are identified and answered with concrete suggestions.

The book concludes by listing general references and resources, both print and electronic, for further reading and learning.

This book does not deal with theories of language acquisition, EAL pedagogy or other relevant elements of working with culturally and linguistically diverse learners. However, we have included some references and resources of relevance, and encourage you to investigate further.

. . . .

CHAPTER ONE

SETTING THE STAGE

To study a mixed group of immigrants is in itself a liberal education.

James S. Woodsworth

For a variety of reasons people from around the world continue to arrive on the shores of North America. People flee from countries wracked by internal political conflict, or which are at war with others; a war's aftermath often generates still further waves of emigrants and refugees. Other reasons for people to flee their homes can include global climate changes that create conditions which make it almost impossible for farmers in certain parts of the world to farm and therefore to sustain themselves. Finally, many people make the difficult decision to leave their country of origin for reasons that have more to do with economic factors than with politics.

Canada and the United States are themselves nations of immigrants, and have received new waves of immigrants and refugees since their earliest days. Today, they remain two of the world's industrialized nations most strongly committed to supporting continued immigration.

Canada

Although the expectation in Canada has been that new arrivals will become part of a multicultural mosaic, a policy outlining the vision of multiculturalism was not clearly articulated until relatively recently. Initial discussion on a policy began in 1971, but the policy itself was not fully implemented until 1988. The Canadian government thereby became the first in the world to create a Multiculturalism Policy.

For years, the Canadian government set the rate of immigration on an annual basis, often in response to turmoil in other parts of the world. As a result, the number of people arriving from year to year tended to fluctuate greatly.

In the early 1990s, however, the federal government started to create a five-year immigration plan that provided for the number of immigrants to grow to 250,000 a year between 1992 and 1995, and to 300,000 annually after that. The goal of this policy was to admit about one per cent of Canada's population each year, provided the country could continue to absorb this number. It should be noted that these figures do not include refugees, as it is extremely difficult to forecast the numbers of people who will choose to seek asylum in any given year.

Since 2001, immigration has ranged between 220,000 and 260,000 immigrants per year. According to *Canada's Immigration Program* of October 2004, Canada has one of the highest per capita immigration rates in the world, and at this point approximately 41% of the people currently living in Canada are either first or second generation immigrants.

In 2010, in terms of top source countries, most immigrants came from various parts of Asia, notably the People's Republic of China, the Philippines and India. These countries are the same top three source countries listed for 2009. Interestingly, though in significantly smaller numbers, the fourth ranking country of immigrants to Canada is the United States, closely followed by the United Kingdom and France.

United States

In the United States, the prevailing philosophy with respect to immigration has always been somewhat different from that of Canada. Immigrants are expected to assimilate into the American "melting pot."

In more recent years, the U.S. has received about a million immigrants a year, a figure that includes an estimated 200,000 illegal immigrants. When illegal immigrants are included in the total, however, the U.S. continues to take in fewer immigrants as a percentage of its population than, for example, Canada or Australia. Nonetheless, the number of people in the United States who do not speak English as a first language continues to grow. For example, over 31 million Hispanics in the U.S. have Spanish as their first language, thus making them the largest linguistic minority group in that nation. As of 2008, immigrants comprised 12.5% (38 million) of the total U.S. population.

Historically, Europe was the main source of much of the migration to North America. This was true during the entire colonial period of both Canada and the United States, and was especially pronounced after the two World Wars. In the second half of the 20th century, however, the number of individuals and families arriving from East and South Asia, the Middle East and Africa has increased, often dramatically. It is no longer unusual to find students from Hong Kong, Chile, Korea, Romania, Iraq and Somalia sitting in the same classroom.

Refugees and Displaced Persons in North America

The stated commitment of both the Canadian and American governments to deal with the issue of refugees and displaced persons has further increased the flow of people to North America—and to our classrooms. In 1994, the United Nations High Commission on Refugees (UNHCR) estimated that the number of refugees and persons of concern worldwide exceeded 19.8 million.

The last few years, however, have again seen a sharp increase in the numbers of refugees, primarily due to the violence in areas of the Middle East and Africa. It is likely that more complex challenges around the world will continue to add to these numbers. What is equally disturbing is that the amount of time spent in refugee camps has increased significantly to an average of 17 years. The sad fact is that UNHCR statistics, reported in 2010, estimated the number of refugees and displaced persons to be at 42 million.

Several countries, including Canada and the United States, are using a "group processing" policy to expedite dealing with the refugee situations in many countries. For example, in efforts to eliminate some refugee camps, we are likely to encounter a sudden influx of Jarai speakers from high in the mountains of central Vietnam. Karen speakers from the camps along the Burma/Thai border have also been arriving, as have some Bhutanese from Nepal.

All recent reports on human migration indicate that the numbers will increase dramatically in the years ahead. The reports also show that the migration is primarily to urban areas where there are already many immigrants from a variety of countries.

The Changing Face of the Classroom

Increasing immigration means that our classrooms are likely to continue welcoming learners whose countries of origin are more and more diverse. We, as teachers, are not necessarily as prepared as we might wish for the arrival of students from various areas of the world.

These new learners bring with them languages, experiences, learning styles and cultural backgrounds that are unfamiliar to most teachers. Unlike English, which uses an alphabetic writing system, some use a pictorial representation system as the basis for written communication. In addition, some languages incorporate a highly stylized tonal system in speech, relying on this to indicate meanings rather than using different words as English typically does.

Some schools are enrolling students who have had little or no previous formal schooling, or whose schooling has been seriously interrupted by political strife. In British Columbia, for example, some 17-years-olds have arrived with as little as two to three years of schooling.

As we welcome new students, we must be careful to keep in mind that there is great diversity within every culture. All the students who arrive from a particular country or with similar cultural backgrounds are not going to exhibit the same traits. We must guard against adopting attitudes based on stereotypes, such as assuming that all Chinese students work hard and are good at mathematics and science. Stereotypes are exactly that: they do not reflect the reality of our classrooms or of the rich diversity of the individuals in them. Sometimes false and/or stereotypical attitudes develop unconsciously, and people remain unaware of their thinking until they are confronted with individuals who do not conform to their preconceived images.

As students from a greater number of countries and backgrounds arrive in our classrooms, our awareness of similarities and differences among groups must increase. Some students come from a background where their schooling has been consistent, while the schooling for others has been interrupted or non-existent. One group tends to speak up in class while another does not. Some feel the need for one correct answer, while others can live with a variety of possible answers.

Working with a wide range of students with diverse linguistic and learning needs forces us to re-evaluate *how* we teach and the assumptions we can and cannot make. In short, it forces us out of our relatively comfortable and predictable ways of teaching. This cannot help but heighten our own levels of anxiety and unease.

At the same time, it is important to remember that students from around the world bring with them complete communication systems, individual differences and rich cultural backgrounds. They are able to function very well in many environments, and the fact that they need assistance with English or adapting to new situations does not suggest that they have inherent learning problems. Too often, it is assumed that these students are deficient—we've all seen people who talk to EAL learners loudly and with exaggerated slowness. (That's not to say, however, that there are not some newly arrived learners who will have unique learning needs. We shall be addressing several of these groups of learners in Chapter Six.)

Most arriving students often need nothing more than time to deal with both learning the language and learning in the language.

It's also worth remembering that not all EAL learners were born outside North America. Some of the students entering our schools were born in Canada or the United States, but learned a language other than English as their first language. They require at least as much attention as, if not more than, EAL speakers from other countries. These students are sometimes caught between two linguistic and cultural worlds, starting school without solid literacy skills in either their home language or English.

Despite the differences among them, EAL learners also share a number of traits. These traits reflect values, attitudes, belief systems, hopes, dreams and aspirations that transcend language. The differences appear to surface in the way these commonalities are expressed or acted upon. Such differences will be explored in some depth in a later chapter.

Culture Shock

One area of commonality among newcomers relates to the adjustment process. Students, parents, peers and teachers must consciously learn to interact and adjust to one another in new ways. Academic, emotional, cultural and social conflicts may arise in school settings.

Since the early 1960s, the phenomenon of "culture shock" has received considerable attention. Simply stated, culture shock encompasses a constellation of feelings and events that occur when we are plunged into an unfamiliar environment. This means the signs and signals of interaction that we have internalized and taken for granted are no longer valid or effective.

Because of traumatic past experiences and factors surrounding their forced arrival, refugees often experience a greater degree of culture shock than immigrants, who have elected to move to a new home country. Because of this, refugees often need more time to work through these inner conflicts. It's worth noting, however, that some immigrant children who had no say in the decision to leave their country of origin may feel anger and resentment about the situation in which they now find themselves. They, too, need time and support to work through their feelings and adjust to their new lives.

Over the years, anthropologists and social psychologists have attempted to increase their understanding of culture shock and its relationship to the settlement and integration processes. Many view culture shock as a series of stages through which individuals pass, sometimes slowly, sometimes in fits and starts, and occasionally, not at all. An awareness and understanding of some of the more obvious stages of culture shock will help us, as teachers, to work more effectively with these new EAL learners. A common way of describing these stages is known as the 4-Hs: Honeymoon; Hostility; Humor; Home. Each is briefly described below.

Stage 1—The Honeymoon. The honeymoon period, usually lasting for up to six months or so, starts when people first arrive. Individuals may demonstrate the following traits:

— Enthusiasm, fascination, and curiosity about their new environment.
— Optimism, excitement and hope for a new and better life.
— Unmistakable foreignness.
— Little identification with their new home country.
— Fatigue.
— Anxiety regarding the future.
— Superficial attempts to adjust.

Stage 2—Hostility. After about four to six months, reality is likely to set in. This is most often the time that culture shock becomes evident. Newcomers know a bit about getting around and have begun to learn how to manage, but where they are now is not like their home: the food, the appearance of things, life itself, places, faces, and ways of doing things are different. Gradually some even feel that they hate their new country, and want to go back home. Individuals may exhibit the following traits:

— Feeling the "strangeness" of school.
— Little verbal communication, except with others who speak their language.
— Slower second language retention.
— Distraction due to unsettled family life or growing family problems.
— Confusion over new social norms and expectations.
— Frustration and possible withdrawal or depression.
— Inexplicable or erratic behaviors.
— Difficulty sitting still.
— Possible cultural disorientation and misunderstandings, both verbal and non-verbal.
— Fear of sharing problems, and challenges of adjustment with others—whether family or friends.

Stage 3—Humor (Coming to Terms). Gradually, newcomers work toward resolution of their feelings and their sense of being torn between the old and the new. They begin to accept their new home and to find friends. They begin to discover that there are good things about where they are living, and come to terms with both the old and new ways of life. Individuals may show the following traits:

— Proficiency in conversational English.
— Disengagement from English as an Additional Language classes/support.
— Peer influence toward or away from various elements of the new society.
— Some attitudinal and values changes.
— Parent-teen conflict due to differences in attitudes may be exaggerated.
— Behavioral problems.
— Improvements in the family's economic situation as at least one parent finds acceptable employment.

Stage 4—Home (Integration). This is the stage at which many students and families realize that they are here to stay. This last stage may take years, and for some will never fully take place.

18

Students may still respond in unexpected ways to particular classroom situations or events, due to cultural conditioning or because their cultural values and beliefs differ from those of other students. Individuals may demonstrate the following traits:

— Comfortable proficiency with English.
— Appreciation of the cultural symbols of both their original and adopted countries.
— Viewing themselves as an integral part of a multicultural society.
— Friendships with individuals from different ethnic origins.
— Participation in school and community activities.
— Acceptance and identification with the host culture, without giving up the original home identity.

These descriptions apply to both immigrant and refugee groups. Often, the length of time it takes to resolve the issues associated with a particular phase marks the only difference in the way stages are experienced by the two groups. It is not uncommon for immigrants to take two to five years to go through the adjustment phases, and for refugees to take between five and 10 years.

Taking the time to find out where EAL learners are on the path of cultural adjustment and consistently communicating with them enables us to find areas of commonality. In this regard, it is important to acknowledge the intimate relationship between culture and communication. Building a successful learning community requires that teachers recognize and incorporate within themselves the knowledge that students will continue to respond in classrooms according to cultural norms and mores learned and absorbed from the day they were born.

Culture

Culture is often viewed as the means of passing on values, perceptions, attitudes and behaviors. Additionally, it is a reflection of tradition, lifestyle and patterned ways of dealing with the world, including unwritten rules for routines as well as rules for work and play. As Edward T. Hall put it in *The Silent Language*: "It is a mold in which we are all cast and it controls our daily lives in many unsuspected ways" (page 30).

The traditional mandate of teachers of new English speakers has been to teach the English language while acquainting these learners with aspects of the host culture. It is being increasingly recognized that developing an awareness and appreciation of the cultural background of the learners can greatly improve teachers' chances of achieving a reasonable measure of success with this task.

For instance, the kind of gestures and language people use to communicate with others is largely determined by culture. In greeting others, people may shake hands, embrace, bow to one another, touch noses, touch the feet of another, or salute. All these are perfectly valid and valued forms of greeting for specific cultural groups; none is universal.

Culture is not innate. It is handed down from adult to child, and this transmission takes place in both formal and informal settings, including school and home. The role-playing of young children provides some useful examples. Suppose you are observing the five-year-olds in a kindergarten class. Watch for examples of social behavior that illustrate the prevailing mores and value systems. See if boys are "allowed" to be the mother when playing house, or if girls are accepted as firefighters. It may surprise you to note the extent of the societal value systems that these young children have already absorbed.

We have deliberately employed the word "absorbed" here because, in many instances, these values have not been specifically taught; rather, they have been observed over time and in a variety of situations. Correct behavior has been positively reinforced, and incorrect behavior criticized in both overt and less obvious ways.

The culture in and of our classrooms relates to both language and behavior. In fact, it is impossible to exclude cultural considerations from our work as teachers. Every day, situations involving cultural differences arise in every classroom. The following chart presents some examples of behavior, typical questions teachers may ask as they interpret the behavior through the filter of their own cultural norms, and possible explanations for the behavior.

Behavior	Question	Possible Explanation
Avoiding eye contact	Why won't you look at me when I talk to you? Are you hiding something?	Downcast eyes show respect
Reluctance to help a peer	Why won't you work with another student?	Ideas about sharing and "owning" knowledge differ
Appearing tired or uninterested	Why are you so tired? What time did you go to bed last night? Are you bored?	Learning a language is hard work; self-regulated bedtime may be the norm
Wearing inappropriate clothing for an activity (e.g. going skating)	Don't you know it's going to be cold here? Where's your sweater?	May not have a range of clothing; unfamiliar with the sport
Wearing inappropriate clothing for the weather	Why do you have on three sweaters?	Feels quite cold even in balmy weather (difference between the home and host countries)
Refusing to eat with peers	Aren't you going to eat your lunch? Did you bring a lunch?	Not used to eating with anyone but family members; worried that their food may provoke ridicule

Behavior	Question	Possible Explanation
Reluctance to answer questions	Didn't you study? Don't you know the answer?	Processing takes time; used to a system in which choral answers are the norm

Because all newcomers bring to their new homelands a wealth of different background experiences, teachers have a multi-faceted task. We must note the differences, acknowledge their validity, create mechanisms to uncover their positive benefits, and incorporate them into our teaching as a way of building bridges among students, and between our students and ourselves.

Given the high probability that an increasingly diverse group of EAL learners will continue to enter our classrooms, how do we prepare ourselves for their arrival? Looking at culture from differing perspectives is a starting point, and is the focus of the next chapter.

Review and Extend

— Consider the range of reasons why people might leave their countries of origin. Make a list and see if you can discover how many reasons are represented in the immigration population at your school.

— When did your ancestors immigrate to North America? What elements of your cultural norms still exist as part of your daily life, rituals, celebrations, and attitudes? Why do you think those elements have remained a valued part of your life? What do they symbolize?

— What stereotypical attitudes have you heard expressed in your work environment or community? How could you respond?

— Have you ever been in a situation in which everything, or nearly everything, was unfamiliar? Reflect on your feelings of that time. What could you do to help learners who may have similar feelings?

— Consider the adjustment stages EAL learners are going through. How might you assist them at any particular stage along the way?

— We don't think of our own culture very often. Make a list of the ways of "being and behaving" you would consider normal. If possible, compare this list with a friend or colleague. Discuss similarities and differences.

CHAPTER TWO

AWARENESS OF CULTURE

Culture is so much an integral part of our life that it is often difficult to realize that there are different, but equally valid, ways of thinking, perceiving and behaving.

Peter Chinn

Our attempts to understand another culture may take many forms—reading about it, viewing travelogues, visiting or living in that context for a period of time. Is there a best way? Probably not. The method we choose depends, in part, on what we mean when we say we "understand" another culture.

It is our belief that an important route to achieving understanding of another culture begins with developing an awareness of our own culture. It is difficult, however, to step back and examine our culture objectively when we are so immersed in it.

The following description of an everyday occurrence in one culture, excerpted from Horace Miner's contribution to *Toward Internationalism: Readings in Cross-Cultural Communication*, pp. 241-246, illustrates this point:

> In the hierarchy of magical practitioners, and below the medicine man in prestige, are specialists whose designation is best translated as "holy mouth men." The Nacirema have an almost pathological horror of and fascination with the mouth, the condition of which is believed to have a supernatural influence on all social relationships. Were it not for the rituals of the mouth, they believe that their teeth would

fall out, their gums bleed, their jaws shrink, their friends desert them, and their lovers reject them. They also believe that a strong relationship exists between oral and moral characteristics. For example, there is a ritual ablution of the mouth for children that is supposed to improve their moral fiber. The daily body ritual performed by everyone includes a mouth rite. Despite the fact that these people are so punctilious about care of the mouth, this rite involves a practice which strikes the uninitiated stranger as revolting. It was reported to me that the ritual consists of inserting a small bundle of hog hairs into the mouth, along with certain magical powders, and then moving the bundle in a highly formalized series of gestures.

Readers will recognize that the ritual simply involves brushing the teeth, but this particular presentation highlights the importance of perspective.

We can conduct our own experiments by looking at ordinary situations from another perspective. For instance, how would you begin to describe driving a car to someone who has never seen a car? How would you describe the car itself? Similarly, how would you describe a computer and its increasingly dazzling capabilities? To someone who has never been to school, how would you describe the organization of the school day? Or how would you describe the movement of classes when the bell rings?

The classic movie *The Gods Must Be Crazy* is a delightful example of the way a particular group reacts to the introduction of a (never-before-seen) foreign object—in this case, a glass Coca Cola bottle—that seems to have fallen from the sky. The story recounts peoples' initial reaction to the bottle, how their treatment of it changes over time, how their interactions with each other begin to shift as a result of the discovery, and their ultimate decision about what to do with the bottle.

In industrialized countries the Coke bottle would quickly be discarded, but the perspective of the group portrayed in the movie was completely different. The bottle was a novelty to be examined and experimented with. The reactions of the characters in this movie demonstrate how much we assume simply because we have never consciously thought about, or questioned, certain ingrained ways of thinking or behaving. In many situations, we take certain behavioral expectations for granted until someone in the group appears to contravene the perceived norm.

For instance, rituals such as greetings can be confusing. When a young man named Manjit, for example, arrived at the airport after a long flight and looked around at how people were interacting, he was understandably dismayed. He was used to greeting people with the traditional *namaste*, which involves making a slight bow while pressing together the palms of the hands chest-high in what might be called a praying position. What he saw were some people shaking hands, others hugging, and some hugging and kissing. The questions that might have run through his mind include:

- — Is this polite behavior in public?
- — Why are different people doing different things?
- — What should I be doing?
- — How do I know what to do?
- — How do I know what's acceptable?
- — Is there a difference in what is appropriate based on my age and gender, and does it vary depending on the person I am greeting?

For Manjit, the *namaste* no longer appeared to be the appropriate and normal form of greeting, but he was confused about what was correct in his new context.

Another example of a ritual we often take for granted is taking turns. During their early years in school, most North American children are taught that taking turns in a systematic fashion is appropriate, valued and correct. In fact, much time and attention is paid to teaching this behavior, and censure can result for those who do not learn it quickly and comply with the norms that have been set out.

Despite all of this training over the years, we do find ourselves in situations in which another person did not wait to take her or his turn. Whether it was while driving or waiting at a grocery store checkout counter, we react. Feelings such as anger and hostility are often engendered at these times, and our reac-

26

tions may range from silent resentment to muttering through clenched teeth to outright public censure of the offender.

Indeed, some people look upon the North American turn-taking courtesies with great dismay. They may wonder how individuals ever accomplish anything or receive any attention at all by acting in a way that they perceive as passive.

In their cultures, it is perfectly acceptable to push, shove, elbow another, or barge in when seeking attention. Seasoned travelers often have tales of times when they temporarily adopted certain unfamiliar cultural ways of being as survival mechanisms, even though they would never dare to exhibit these same behaviors in North America.

When children from such cultures arrive in North American classrooms, it is all too easy to form hasty judgments about what these students are like. These judgments reflect one value system, but may show an inadequate understanding and lack of tolerance for the different values and behaviors of other cultural groups.

At the beginning of this chapter, we stated that becoming aware of one's own culture is an important starting point for understanding other cultures. L. Robert Kohls, the Executive Director of the Washington International Center, created a highly useful model to assist with this process. In his work with international visitors to the United States, he outlined in chart form what he felt were 13 core American values and juxtaposed them with contrasting orientations that might well be much more representative of other cultural groups. His intent was to help foreign students and other visitors understand the how and why of seemingly puzzling North American behavior—"to look at Americans through the eyes of our visitors." We have adapted his chart, as it provides a helpful window on the values and perspectives many of us share.

Kohls' chart provides one interesting tool that can help us begin to think about cultural values. It does not suggest that all people in North America—or elsewhere—hold one set of values and not another; rather, each characteristic should be viewed as located on a continuum. We can use this to identify where we would place ourselves on each continuum. It can also be used as a tool to help you and your students determine their viewpoints.

Values in North America	Values in Other Cultures
Personal control over environment, responsibility	Fate, destiny
Change is natural and positive	Stability, tradition, continuity
Time and its control	Human interaction
Equality, fairness	Hierarchy, rank, status
Individualism, independence	Group welfare, dependence
Self-help, initiative	Birthright, inheritance
Competition	Cooperation
Future orientation	Past orientation
Action, work orientation	"Being" orientation
Informality	Formality
Directness, openness, honesty	Indirectness, ritual, saving face
Practicality, efficiency	Idealism, theory
Materialism, acquisitiveness	Spiritualism, detachment

A great deal of the cross-cultural research begun in more recent decades was motivated by finding ways to enhance our efforts to "do business" around the world. Given today's global economy, knowing how to "make a deal" across cultures would certainly be an asset.

You will recognize the underlying principles of Hofstede's five dimensions, as they are also reflected in Kohl's work as noted above. Hofstede, a noted Dutch social psychologist and anthropologist, has explored them in much more depth and across different social strata within a number of cultures and countries. His efforts to look at how values are influenced by culture are focused on the following five dimensions:

- *Power Distance Index*. While all societies have a power and equality differential, in North America considerable effort is made to downplay these differences in status. How a particular group values that distance is highly variable.
- *Individualism*. Are individuals expected to look after themselves (and immediate family members) or are they trained from birth to be unquestioningly loyal to and to consider the collective, including extended families across the generations, to be of primary importance?
- *Masculinity*. Masculinity is usually equated with dominance and assertiveness, while the more modest and caring societies are considered more feminine.
- *Uncertainty Avoidance Index*. To what extent does a group feel comfortable, or not, with the open-ended and ambiguous, as opposed to the strictly rule-governed and predictable?
- *Long Term Orientation*. Thrift and perseverance are key elements of this orientation. At the opposite end of the continuum would be a lack of concern over meeting obligations and respecting cultural traditions.

What struck us in this research are some of the markedly different responses given by different culture/country groups. It is perhaps no surprise that the United States and Canada, as well as the United Kingdom and Australia, are among the seven countries that rate the Individualism dimension as by far the highest of all 70 countries represented.

Conversely, these same countries rank Long Term Orientation as significantly lower than the average across all countries. Perhaps the extreme end of this continuum would be the "Now" mindset that pervades advertising today, where much is made of immediate gratification. One might wonder what this says about how we would deal with those inclined toward the other end of these two continua.

How is this relevant to our work with learners who represent a wide range of orientations along these continua? Consider some sample scenarios and consider how our current schooling system would tend to react.

— A student has been frequently absent due to "family reasons." It is discovered that this is, in fact, due to the illness of a younger sibling, and that the parents cannot take time off from work. Getting a babysitter or a neighbor to look after the sick child is not considered an acceptable option.

— End-of-term projects are outlined in class. It is made clear that students can choose one (from the list provided) that appeals to them personally, and they are encouraged to be creative in their approach and final presentation. After initially receiving some one-to-one assistance to choose a project, an EAL learner persists in asking questions about details of the assignment at every opportunity. He's clearly extremely anxious about doing the right thing.

— Ms. Walters has encouraged and reminded her new EAL learners that students are to call their teachers by their first names, a long-standing tradition at her school. However, one student persists in addressing her as "Teacher," as does his mother when she comes to pick him up after class. Ms. Walters is trying hard not to be annoyed by this persistence and seeming lack of acceptance of what she feels is simply a very friendly approach to newcomers.

Each scenario is an example of an appropriate response to the situation—appropriate, that is, from the perspective of someone raised with a specific cultural mindset—yet a mindset that is not considered the expected response within our classrooms and schools.

What this chapter has emphasized is that we are the products of our cultural upbringing, the explicit and implicit training that proceeds from the day our first responses to our parents are reinforced in ways that validate our cultural ways of being. In attempting to understand other cultures, it is important to begin with our own because we can develop greater understanding of our own background and the overt and covert forces that shape it. In other words, there can be a better understanding of self.

The greater your understanding of your own personal preferences, the more able you will be to notice and potentially work with your learners to create a learning space that is, if not always comfortable, at least more acceptable for all. Your heightened awareness will help EAL learners function more successfully in their new culture and language, while at the same time enriching the understandings of their non-EAL peers.

Now that you have taken the time to consider your own personal perspective, the next chapter provides an introduction to EAL learners—a collective that is, however, culturally and linguistically unique.

Review and Extend

— Ask yourself how you greet various people within your personal and professional spheres. Why? What do these greetings reveal about the extent and depth of various relationships? How have your greeting patterns changed over time?

— What do you notice about the way(s) in which your students greet each other? What do these various approaches lead you to surmise about their relationships?

— Even the tone of voice used when speaking the formulaic "Hello" has implied meaning. When we hear a particular tone, we make assumptions about the mindset of the speaker. How do we know if our assumptions are correct?

— What is it about taking turns that makes it so important? What associations are there with taking turns? Courtesy? Order? Fairness? Organization? Symmetry? Purpose? Power? All these, and more? Discuss these thoughts with a colleague. How similar are your perceptions?

— What associations accompany a failure to take turns? Disorganization? Chaos? Inability to control? The weaker members of the group being pushed aside and/or excluded? A poor reflection on the abilities of classroom teachers to maintain order? Consider comparing your thoughts with others.

— For each characteristic mentioned in Kohls' chart, think about where you would locate yourself on the continuum. If you are close to one end and you suspect that students in your class(es) are closer to the other, this may present challenges in terms of how smoothly interaction and, indeed, learning itself, will occur.

CHAPTER THREE

EAL LEARNERS ARE

INDIVIDUALS

To speak another's language without understanding the culture is to make a fluent fool of oneself.

Edward T. Hall

The metaphor of an iceberg is often used to illustrate culture (please refer to Chapter Seven for more details.) The small visible portion of the iceberg above the water line includes physical characteristics, distinctive styles of clothing, food, art and, of course, language. It is also relatively easy to learn a bit more about the previous schooling background of the new learners and a little of the social milieu in which they have been living until now.

The much larger portion below the waterline, however, includes many aspects of communication that are grounded in the various values and beliefs we all hold. These are culturally determined. For example, our perceptions of what constitutes polite behavior in specific situations is based on what we have been taught is the right way to behave in particular situations. How we judge cleanliness and punctuality are rooted in the values we hold about these manifestations of who we are. Censure may not be verbal, but our approval or disapproval is made manifest in a variety of ways. It is these less visible, and often nonverbal, aspects of culture that, to a large extent, define our behavior toward and the ways we communicate with others.

33

The overriding purpose of this book is to illustrate how inextricably culture and communication are interwoven. This chapter will examine a number of the surface aspects of the cultural iceberg, highlighting some of the crucial cultural variables that relate to who EAL learners are and how this affects their interactions with other individuals in general, and with teachers and fellow learners in particular.

It has been said that culture is communication and communication is culture. When discussing culture and communication, we must always keep in mind that we are dealing with individuals. Though members of any cultural group share certain culturally influenced behaviors and styles of interacting, we all have our own idiosyncrasies, motivations and personal styles. In fact, we all are members of several cultures, not only one.

Belonging to Several Cultures

Matthew is in his 12th year of schooling, attending a special high school program in an upper middle class neighborhood. This program for self-motivated learners includes enrichment activities that range from participation in nation-wide mathematics competitions and science laboratory work at the nearby university, to rock-climbing expeditions and ski-camp retreats.

When we read this, we may form an immediate impression of this young man. For example, we take it for granted that he's bright, that he comes from a well-to-do family that lives in an urban setting, and that he has had opportunities many other students will never have.

In reality, however, Matthew rides the bus for more than an hour every day to get to school because his family cannot afford to live in the fairly expensive housing near the school. He wears secondhand clothing, has no specialized equipment and works part-time to help support his attendance at this school. He lacks the money to participate in the more exotic activities offered at the school, and knows that he needs to win a scholarship if he is to go on to higher education.

To which culture does Matthew belong? Several. He belongs to the working class of a large urban center. His German mother has influenced his taste in food and music with some ethnic aspects of her own culture. He associates with students who, like him, do not live in the school's catchment area and whose socio-economic background may or may not be the same as his. He is a strict vegetarian—placing him in a somewhat trendy cultural group—and aspires to be a music teacher, which exposes him to two more cultural groups, teachers in general and music teachers in particular. Teachers and parents of teenagers will know that Matthew also belongs to a powerful teen cultural group that grown-ups sometimes have difficulty understanding.

The initial, superficial description of Matthew may have led us to make a particular set of assumptions about who he is. As information about his heritage and circumstances was added, it became necessary to reassess, sometimes several times, our picture of him. We are all the products of a variety of influences: our heritage, lifestyle, economic circumstances and age group, to mention a few. Therefore, we all belong to several cultural groups, though not all are necessarily clearly definable and many overlap, at least to some extent.

Cultural Assumptions

Judging students on the basis of the superficial description applied to Matthew is shortsighted and can be quite damaging. Yet this has often been the case. As teachers, we need to be aware of the possible conflicts that might arise when, with the best possible intentions, we encourage student-to-student interactions and foster communicative relationships. The following points serve to illustrate some of the challenges we may face.

COMMON HOME LANGUAGE

When a new non-English-speaking student comes into a school, a prudent first step is to find someone else in the school, grade or class who speaks the same first language. This buddy can help the new student become familiar with routines and regulations, and can ease the transition into the new environment.

While this is a good idea, care must be taken not to make inappropriate assumptions by disregarding particulars of the students' backgrounds that may seriously affect this relationship that has been imposed upon them.

For example, while the new student and the buddy may speak the same first language, there may be little understanding between them on any other level. They could, in fact, come from areas that have been sworn enemies for centuries. At the very least, they are the products of their own unique heritage and the circumstances that have brought them to their present situation.

SOCIO-ECONOMIC STATUS

Relative social or economic status—factors that are often played down in North American society—may be of vital importance for given individuals and their cultural groups, and may also make it difficult for assigned buddies to relate to each other. A child from a wealthy family who has never known hunger or deprivation is unlikely readily to see eye-to-eye with a recent immigrant from a refugee camp or a war-torn country, nor will she or he understand the needs and priorities of someone raised on a subsistence farm. In some cases, the children of subsistence farmers are less likely to have had access to formal schooling than even poor children from cities. Both these groups are unlikely to understand the intense focus often placed on education by well-to-do families.

Groups of children from three very different social, political and economic backgrounds may all speak the same language, but they will operate at very different levels within a North American school system. Assign buddies, by all means, but use this strategy with care.

RELIGION

Another factor that must be considered is religion. Both history and the contemporary world abound with examples of strife caused by differences in religious beliefs and practices. Examples include historical strife from the Crusades to the more recent troubles in Ireland and the continuing struggles between Sikhs and Hindus in India and Pakistan, and Christians and Muslims in many parts of the world. Again, new students to the school may carry the same country's passport and speak the same first language, yet be worlds apart on religious grounds.

GENDER

Perhaps the most basic aspect of personal differences is gender. No one would deny that gender plays an important role in defining the way people communicate with each other. Nonetheless, in the typical North American classroom where teachers attempt to treat everyone equally, considerable energy is expended in attempting to erase gender as a contributing factor in communication.

In treating all students equally and encouraging them to do likewise with each other, we may be denying a reality that all the students already know as a result of their cultural learning outside the classroom and in the home. As we struggle valiantly to ensure equality of access to education for boys and girls, members of one cultural group laud us. At the same time, members of other cultural groups, who believe these efforts undermine the principles and gender-based traditions of their way of life, may disparage us.

We may also create discomfort if we attempt to buddy up a new student, for orientation purposes, with a member of the opposite sex. If the new student is female, she may be too embarrassed to ask questions of her male buddy and, if the roles are reversed, the new male student may feel insulted to have been assigned a female guide, common language notwithstanding.

Other challenges may arise. One example concerns the fact that it is by default the girls from a number of cultures who have to stay home from school to help with younger siblings. On the other hand, the boys from a particular cultural group may warn girls from the same background—in their first language—to keep quiet in class and make no demands on the teacher's time because such forwardness is considered unseemly and is the prerogative of the male members of the class.

Through the eyes of a member of the dominant culture in North America, these actions seem to impinge on the rights of the girls. It is important to remember that this conclusion results from viewing the incidents from one cultural perspective only. This particular point was driven home in a recent interview with a married woman from a culture in which arranged marriages are the norm. Most North Americans see this lack of freedom of choice on the part of the female as unacceptable.

What this young woman made clear is that, although she understood our desire to have what in her culture is called a "love marriage," she wished to point out the many advantages of an arranged marriage, including her own.

First of all, she said that no one knows you better than your parents—and they are also likely to know a great deal about the husband-to-be. Second, your parents are more likely to think clearly about whether the match will be a good one because they are not involved emotionally as one is when "in love." And, finally, she pointed out that there is some room to express personal reactions and opinions when the two betrothed begin to meet formally.

In addition, she cited the high divorce rate in North America as well as the high number of single-parent women living below the poverty line. This is almost unheard of when marriages are arranged. In this situation, women are protected and looked after virtually for life—even if the husband dies, the woman "belongs" to his extended family and remains their responsibility, continuing to live with them and be part of that group.

This young woman was by no means the downtrodden chattel it would be easy to envision when we take the stereotypical view of arranged marriages. In fact, she was well educated, knowledgeable and articulate about both her personal cultural norms and those of English-speaking society. (This is, incidentally, another instance when education plays a role. The situation of an uneducated woman from a rural village in the same country might be somewhat different. However, the interviewee's points are well taken.)

In North America, the style of dress often tends to minimize gender differences. Unless students attend a school where uniforms are the norm, clothing tends to be very casual and definitely unisex. Both boys and girls wear jeans, T-shirts and runners or a variation on this theme. This style may seem somewhat casual to new immigrant parents, though it is not necessarily a major concern.

Style of dress may, however, become more of a concern in gym classes, one of the few areas in the public school system where some sort of uniform is often required, usually shorts, T-shirts and runners. While this dress code has been adopted for a variety of good reasons—freedom of movement and coolness amongst others—it is looked upon with consternation by parents of girls from many cultures.

Changing in front of strangers is bad enough, but the unseemly exposure of the legs—whether classes are co-ed or not—and the expectation that a shower will be taken when the class ends are tantamount to blasphemy. With Muslim girls (and traditional Sikh boys) an additional challenge concerns the need to keep the head covered. This has raised safety concerns for contact sports. As a result, teachers may receive a continual stream of requests to excuse students from participating in gym classes or find that they are simply absent on days when physical education is scheduled.

In many cultures, girls and women customarily dress and interact in extremely modest ways, are usually accompanied by chaperones, and never interact with the opposite sex except in formal settings or in the strictest privacy if they are married. It is not difficult to imagine how distressed these girls—and their families—would be when placed in co-educational classes. This is a cultural norm that is very different, and which must be recognized and dealt with appropriately rather than ignored. It is not difficult simply to seat students of each gender together, including activity groupings, until all are feeling more able to work in new groupings.

Gender, together with age, also plays a vital role in defining teacher-student relationships. Though some measure of respect for elders is taught to North American youth, a healthy skepticism and reasoned questioning of any form of authority is tolerated and, indeed, encouraged. As teachers, we cultivate students' ability to think for themselves on matters of importance while, at the same time, demanding respect for and attention to what we consider important elements of education and curriculum. This rather mixed message has resulted in some problems in our public school system; nevertheless, we tend to value reasoned dissent more than obedience.

When students from other cultures enter this milieu, they attempt to interact based on the beliefs and values about education developed in their own cultures. In many cultures education is, first of all, a privilege that is not to be abused in any way. In these cultures teachers, as adults and educated individuals, are respected and even revered. It is considered the height of insolence and disrespect to question anything the teacher says or does. (Please see Chapter Five for further discussion of this issue.)

Imagine the confusion of students from these particular backgrounds when the teacher almost demands discussion and questioning—and when some students indeed respond by questioning and challenging the teacher's knowledge and authority.

PREVIOUS SCHOOLING

A variety of other factors can also create conflict and misunderstandings. For instance, if student access to formal schooling in their home country has been limited, teachers may encounter teenaged students who have never attended school of any sort, though this by no means implies that they are "uneducated."

In fact, they may have been forced to survive in extreme circumstances, living by their wits if they were to survive at all. In the same class, there may be other students from the same cultural background who have attended school from a very young age. These two groups may have only two things in common: they speak the same first language and they do not speak English.

All the above examples show that simply sharing a language does not ensure smooth communication or indicate like-mindedness among EAL students any more than it does among native English speakers. A number of factors including gender, religion, historical traditions, age and socio-economic status, can influence an individual's identity. To facilitate communication, teachers will have significantly more success if they take such differences into account.

This is the reality teachers face working with students from a wide variety of backgrounds. Students may view the process of education and each other in very different ways from what we might be tempted to assume; yet they may, at the same time, look to us to help them find their way in the new—and sometimes strange—culture and language in which they find themselves suddenly immersed.

If we consider the historical, cultural, socio-economic, age and gender factors, it will go a long way toward building a better understanding among cultural groups. However, despite everybody's best intentions and even with a reasonable command of the target language, cultural differences in styles of communication can confound these efforts. Communication beyond language, beyond the actual words spoken, will be the topic of the next chapter.

Review and Extend

— Think about the many cultural groups to which you belong. In addition to your ethnic heritage, these may include groups based on your gender, your marital status, whether you have siblings, and whether you grew up in or outside a city. Too often we describe ourselves according to a single definition, when the reality is that we are influenced by many factors, including many that are culture-based.

— Involve some colleagues in doing the exercise above. Compare notes.

41

— Your students also belong to several cultures. As a class activity, have them write down the cultures to which they belong, and then encourage them to discuss these with a partner, either from the same or from a different culture, to establish the similarities and the differences.

— In this chapter, arranged marriage was used as an example of cultural differences. Think of another example of a cultural difference, and then explore it in greater detail through conversations with colleagues or through research.

— As you work with your students, reflect on friendships and who talks with whom. What factors may be influencing student decisions about choices regarding friendships and those with whom they choose to communicate?

— How do you create ways for students to participate in classroom routines, tasks and communication activities?

  • Are your instructions explicit and clear, or do you sometimes assume a level of background knowledge that EAL learners do not yet possess?

  • In thinking about classroom/group tasks, do you include ways for EAL learners to participate and demonstrate their understandings nonverbally?

. . . .

CHAPTER FOUR

EAL LEARNERS AND

COMMUNICATION

If verbal communication is the pen which spells out details,
nonverbal communication provides the surface on which the
words are written and against which they must be interpreted.

Earl Stevick

For a long time, conventional North American
wisdom suggested that communicating between cultures simply
involved learning the language of the other. As a result, the
teaching methods employed were heavily based on the linguistic
methods used to train diplomats for work in service overseas. It
is now clear that, while speaking a language certainly paves the
way, simply knowing the words is not nearly enough to
facilitate optimal communication. Rather, language can serve as
a bridge to facilitate a deeper understanding.

With this chapter, we have reached the point where we're
ready to delve below the surface of the metaphorical waters
mentioned in the previous chapter to examine the submerged
portion of the cultural iceberg. This portion refers to the less
concrete, often hidden aspects of culture, which manifest
themselves as actions and behaviors. Why, for instance, do male
members of some cultural groups hug and kiss when greeting
one another in public, while members of another group display
no touching behavior of any sort and, in a third, only females
exhibit this kind of physical closeness?

Actions—or lack of actions—can spark a variety of responses,
ranging from mere puzzlement to open hostility. The way

people communicate with others is an important element of culture and is governed by communication styles, attitudes, values and belief systems. These aspects of culture are rule-governed and quite specific and explicit, *but only to those born and raised in that particular culture.* Additionally, there is no rule book or explicit set of instructions. Instead, from a very early age, children absorb the culturally appropriate way to communicate and/or are provided with positive reinforcement to validate their growing ability to "act like one of us."

The most obvious component of communication is language. This book assumes that using language to communicate forms the basis for what goes on in the classroom. In addition, however, the way other forms of communication are used is discussed in some detail because these less obvious aspects illustrate cultural differences that may affect not only the verbal but also the overall communication efforts.

We have divided the discussion of these aspects of communication into three areas: coverbal communication, nonverbal communication, and values and belief systems. The first two—coverbal and nonverbal communication—will be discussed in this chapter. However, because values and belief systems are the complex basis upon which all other communication is founded, Chapter Seven will deal exclusively with this aspect of communication.

Keep in mind that this division is useful only for illustrating and clarifying issues. In fact, all three of these aspects of communication interact in both overt and subtle ways to create a style that is culturally based and grounded in firmly held values and beliefs.

Coverbal Communication

In North America, the coverbal and nonverbal aspects of communication have received considerable attention over the last few decades. Researchers have argued that the verbal component of any single act of communication between members of the *same* cultural group may comprise as little as seven per cent of the act, while the rest consists of coverbal and nonverbal elements. Even if this percentage is somewhat extreme, it goes a long way toward explaining why simply knowing a language does not guarantee smooth cross-cultural relationships.

Coverbal behavior, also known as paralanguage, includes all aspects of voice modification in speech and any vocalizations used in listening. For instance, think about the way you listen to a friend describe an experience. As you're listening, you punctuate the tale with comments such as, "Wow!" "You're kidding!" "Uh huh," and so on. This is coverbal behavior. It demonstrates that you are listening and following the story closely, reacting emotionally to and "cooperating with" the speaker.

In some Asian cultures, however, this kind of coverbal feedback does not indicate comprehension. The vocalization, and the head nodding that often accompanies it, indicates only that the listener is giving the speaker her or his full attention, as is polite.

As teachers, we tend to interpret this kind of coverbal behavior (especially if it is accompanied by head nodding) as an indication of comprehension. The listener seems to be saying, "Yes, yes, I understand. I get it." In fact, this is often not the case, as we discover later when the students in question demonstrate their lack of understanding of the task at hand.

At this point, we may feel frustrated and somewhat duped by the students who gave every indication—according to our accepted norms of behavior—that they understood the task and believed themselves capable of completing it. This is an assumption we must try to avoid.

Our precise coverbal behavior varies with the speaker, the story being told, where the story is being told, and the nature of the relationship between the speaker and the listener. In addition, as indicated previously, coverbal behavior is culture-based. In some cultural groups, extensive coverbal feedback while listening may not be considered appropriate at all, or may depend on the relative status, gender and age of the participants.

When we are speaking, our coverbal behavior also involves how we say what we say. Take the following sentence, for example:

"I wouldn't do that if I were you."

In this sentence, we can change the significance of what we're saying by shifting the emphasis. For example, we could place the emphasis on the two occurrences of "I" as opposed to emphasizing the word "do." In fact, we could go through the entire sentence and, by merely shifting the emphasis, change the intended message. As teachers, we have all used our voices to communicate something beyond the actual words being said, whether this is to warn, give hints, challenge or remain maddeningly neutral.

Intonation is another aspect of coverbal behavior, one that has been studied extensively, not only within cultures but also across cultures, particularly with respect to how differences in intonation patterns can cause miscommunication. This is another example of a situation in which simply knowing the language is not enough to ensure effective communication. Linguistic anthropologists, as well as discourse analysts, have studied this aspect of coverbal behavior (also known as prosodic communication) extensively, and have pointed out the real problems that can arise. Individuals who, to all intents and purposes, speak the same language but come from different cultural backgrounds, can seriously misconstrue their intentions because their intonation patterns are different.

Another aspect of intonation is tone. Most Asian languages are tonal languages, which means that the same word uttered in a different tone can convey an entirely different meaning. When we consider that some languages have nine or more tones, this becomes a very complex and important aspect of communication.

In English, tone is used to convey feelings, not to change the meaning of words in the literal sense. We have all heard and used this device in our communication, though sometimes we may not be entirely conscious of doing so. The sentence cited earlier demonstrates that varying emphasis is an element of coverbal behavior that highlights this use of tone.

Saying, "I wouldn't do that if I were you," with the tonal emphasis on both occurrences of "I" may convey feelings such as censure (You sure are stupid to do that!), a condescending assessment of an action (Some people simply don't know how to do things properly!), or a difference of opinion leading to an alternative suggestion for possible actions. Defining which of these three messages—or which combination of the three—is intended depends on the context, the identity of the participants in the exchange and the nature of their relationship with each other.

Although this use of coverbal communication behavior is fairly well understood, many do not realize that children who perceive a conflict between the verbal message and the nonverbal or coverbal aspect of the same message interpret the nonverbal message as the truth, the "real" message.

Because children are still learning how to act and interact, they are likely to give the coverbal, as well as the nonverbal, message the worst possible connotation. In other words, instead of interpreting the message in the example as, "I'll help you do this a better way," they are likely to interpret it as, "You're so stupid. You can't do anything right." The potential for eroding the self-esteem of learners is painfully obvious.

For these reasons, we must be very conscious of how we use tone to convey meaning in the classroom. What we might consider a "just kidding" or obviously sarcastic use of language, and accompanying exaggerated tone, could easily be interpreted as quite negative, due to the lack of understanding of the context and cultural differences embedded in the utterance. For EAL learners, who are having enough difficulty in just figuring out what the words themselves mean, interpreting tone adds a hidden level of complexity that makes their task even more difficult.

Nonverbal Communication

Nonverbal communication or behavior is much more than simply "not words." It occurs largely out of conscious awareness, is pervasive in our daily communication with others, and is culture-based. In other words, the way we illustrate our words is specific to our culture and is related to culture-specific values and belief systems.

The power of the nonverbal components of communication cannot be overestimated. At some time or other, everyone has likely walked into a room and known instantly, without hearing any talk or seeing any specific interactions taking place, that something is amiss. How do we know? Because thousands of minute signals that are below our conscious level of awareness tell us so.

In this situation, we may act upon our unconscious, almost instinctive, knowledge by either withdrawing, if we feel like an intruder or outsider, or by asking what is wrong, if we wish to get involved or help in some way. As teachers, we often encounter the aftermath of incidents like this in the classroom or on the playground. Though nothing is said, the atmosphere is heavy with unspoken communication.

In general, nonverbal communication includes the kind of coverbal behavior outlined previously, as well as kinesics, proxemics, haptics and artifacts, which are each explained in detail below. Silence and time are also important elements of nonverbal communication. When we present ourselves to others, we combine these elements to convey our feelings and attitudes; we use them to "illustrate" the words we are saying.

KINESICS

Kinesics, a term coined by Ray Birdwhistell, includes all bodily movement—posture, gesture, eye contact and so on—that is an integral part of the communication process. His minute analysis of body movement pioneered research into this area of nonverbal communication: we now know that our bodily movements can have a lesser or greater impact on communication. Indeed it has been said that we cannot *not* communicate in the presence of another.

One subcategory of kinesics is the use of gestures, a familiar part of everyday interaction and one that teachers often rely upon. Visualize yourself in your classroom, for example. Johnny is off task and chatting to a friend at the pencil sharpener. You catch his eye, frown slightly, shake your head and point to his seat. If both you and the child are from the dominant North American culture, the message is clear to both of you. Signals like this are part of the daily routine of communication in the classroom.

At the same time, teachers need to be aware that the meaning of signals like this won't necessarily be clear to students from other cultures. For her MA research, Sylvia studied a group of three- and four-year-olds whose first languages were other than English. She determined that many typical gestures used by teachers fail to transmit the intended message when they are used in the classroom. Rather, as noted earlier, since our nonverbal behavior is culture-based, gestures can be as linguistically different as languages.

In addition, because this research was conducted with very young learners, it also became abundantly clear that nonverbal behavior is learned very early and is, by implication, well entrenched by the time teachers encounter EAL learners in their classrooms.

An EAL teacher related the classic example of gestures being completely misunderstood by us. She had taken her class of EAL teenagers on an outing. In an attempt to call them together in a public place, she used the well-known Western gesture, palm up and curling the fingers towards herself.

To her consternation, a group of them turned their backs and began to disperse rather than move closer. She called them by name while continuing to gesture and saw confusion on their faces. Eventually, they responded to her verbal calls and gathered round.

She had unwittingly given these teens a mixed message. Her words indicated that she wanted them to come closer but her gesture was interpreted as "get going/move away." No wonder they looked confused! Much later, she discovered that the gesture needed to gather this group was palm down while waving the joined fingers, rather than palm up. A simple thing like this can not only cause misunderstanding and confusion, but also create the mistaken perception that the students are being deliberately disobedient.

Miscommunication on the nonverbal level is, by its nature, far more difficult to correct than spoken words. If we don't understand the words, we can always ask the speaker to clarify or repeat. It would be extremely odd, however, to ask what someone meant by, for example, frowning, rolling the eyes and a sudden exhalation of breath.

In addition, nonverbal communication often takes place outside our conscious awareness. As a result, questioning the nonverbal behavior of a speaker is difficult. In the first place, we get a message beyond the words without being clear about how or why we do so. In the second place, we are interpreting the nonverbal element of the communication from our own cultural base—our own value and belief system—which has led us to act and interact in a particular way in a given setting.

Before leaving the topic of gestures, two caveats are appropriate. Attempting to learn the appropriate gestures for all the cultures represented in a multicultural classroom is unrealistic. Not only is it a gargantuan task, (especially because the clientele may change over the course of the school year), but the use of gestures is also dependent on the context.

For the same reasons, it is a good idea to be cautious about using recipe-like books that purport to enable us to "read a person like a book." For example, scratching the side of the nose has been identified as a demonstration of disbelief in what the speaker is saying. What happens if the listener simply has an itchy nose? Books such as this do not address the context of the interaction, and the interpretations given are also decidedly culture-based.

Experience has taught us that two very common gestures in Western culture are worth avoiding with EAL students. The first is the circled thumb and forefinger to indicate approval and the second is the raised and crossed index and middle finger to indicate that we are wishing someone good luck. Both these gestures have a variety of meanings in other cultures, most of them seriously negative, slanderous or of a sexual nature. For these reasons, it would be prudent to avoid them whenever possible!

Eye contact is another common example of culturally different kinesic behavior that is tied strongly to values and belief systems, which will be discussed in a later chapter. For the moment, it is important to note that Western culture pays very careful attention to eye contact. A listener who is honest and engaged makes frequent, though intermittent, eye contact with the speaker during a conversation. On the other hand, constant eye contact—staring—conveys a completely different message.

For example, teachers using North American norms of behavior tend to feel certain that if a listener refuses to make eye contact she or he is, at the least, not attending or, at worst, devious and/or "guilty as charged." This is a value judgment based on cultural norms of nonverbal behavior in given situations. In many cultures, however, frequent eye contact, particularly between an adult and a younger person, is considered the height of rudeness, if not a show of outright hostility and a challenge to the authority of the adult.

As a result, a student who is behaving in a manner appropriate to her or his culture by keeping eyes to the ground and listening in silence can mistakenly be labeled as shifty, guilty, dishonest, disinterested or sulky. Who has not heard an exasperated teacher proclaim, "Look at me when I talk to you!" Ironically, in some cultures expressing rudeness has to do with directing the soles of the feet toward the speaker. Eye contact has nothing to do with it at all.

Clearly, these examples illustrate that it is important for teachers to be careful about assuming that the meaning they attribute to a particular gesture is the same as that of the students. In fact, trying not to make assumptions and, when they are made, checking out the conclusions drawn should be the mandate of teachers wishing to limit communication breakdowns.

PROXEMICS

Proxemics has to do with the use of personal space, the physical distance we place between others and ourselves. The relative placement of physical objects and the use of physical space on a larger scale are also considered to be elements of proxemic behavior. Edward T. Hall, the cultural anthropologist and prolific writer, who has written several volumes on aspects of nonverbal communication differences across cultures, sees all use of space as culture-based.

A North American example of proxemics could be illustrated in this way. Imagine going to get on a bus at the end of a long day to find there is only one other passenger on the bus, a stranger to you, already seated. Would you choose to sit beside this stranger? Likely not. What would be the reaction if you did choose to sit right beside her or him? This common occurrence and the rules about where you choose to sit are seldom examined for their cultural significance.

To bring its significance closer to our daily work, picture the layout of your classroom. Where is your desk located and how are students' desks or tables arranged? In rows? In groups? Lined up squarely with walls or askew?

The way your classroom is laid out and the way you create space for interaction in the classroom is, in part, a reflection of your preferences with respect to the size of your own "personal space bubble." Some of us need to keep our own space—for example, the desk—inviolable and inaccessible, while others freely share this space.

Arrangements such as this are often a nonverbal statement of how physically close individuals are inviting others to come. Obviously, sitting across a large desk from someone is more formal than sitting side by side on the same side of the desk. And sitting in student desks across from or beside each other is more formal than sitting on a couch or in other side-by-side-orientations.

In terms of actual physical contact, those who have taught young children know that some are very physically demonstrative, frequently hugging each other and you, while others appear stand-offish and do not like to be touched. This is a reflection of who they are and how big they prefer their personal space bubble to be.

We all use space to regulate our relationships with others. We can keep people at a distance, both physically and metaphorically or, alternatively, demonstrate positive feelings by drawing someone closer.

Again, this may or may not be done at a conscious level, but the action—or actions—will speak volumes. Great dissonance can therefore be created when a teacher, who feels her personal space is being violated, repeatedly rebuffs a child from a culture in which displays of physical affection are the norm.

As with all nonverbal communication, proxemic behavior, though governed to an extent by individual preference, is also culture-specific. In fact, the tendency is to react to a perceived invasion of personal space at an almost unconscious level, which can create immediate dissonance and miscommunication.

In the homes of many native English-speakers, for instance, it is common for children to have their own bedrooms from a very young age. In fact, one of the ways parents signal respect for their children's physical and personal space is by knocking on their bedroom door rather than simply walking in.

In a number of cultures in which physical and personal space are more likely to be shared, the custom of giving children their own rooms is considered cold and unfeeling. Though closer living arrangement may simply reflect economic and space issues, the cultural predisposition toward a physically closer style is also part of the equation.

Finally, it must be noted that proxemic behavior is also related to values and belief systems. Gender, age, setting, relationship and status are key variables of proxemic behavior and will be discussed in a later chapter.

HAPTICS

Haptics refers to all touching behavior, from a light tap on the shoulder to the slap or "high five" athletes give each other after a particularly good play during a competition. Obviously, haptics is closely related to proxemics; it is not possible to touch someone, even inadvertently, if they keep themselves isolated in a large personal space bubble.

In the classroom, however, some 30 or so students and one adult spend many hours in closer proximity than may normally be preferred by individual members of that group. In addition, it is quite common for teachers to touch students, particularly younger ones, to guide, or to show concern, approval or simple appreciation. This, too, can give rise to cultural conflict and misunderstanding.

Unfortunately, children who feel uncomfortable with this kind of touching often don't express their feelings because they are reluctant to appear to be challenging the authority figure, the teacher. As a result, to save undue stress and discomfort for both the students and ourselves, we should be aware of some of the cultural bases of these behaviors.

In primary classrooms, it is not uncommon for the teacher to hug children, give a pat on the head, shoulder or back, or simply take them firmly by the hand and lead them somewhere. As students grow older, this kind of touching usually becomes less frequent, depending on the individual teacher and student and also on the personal space comfort zone of each. School policy may also affect attitudes toward touching.

However, for people from some cultures, even incidental touching in certain areas such as the head or a handshake between the sexes is perceived to be a personal violation, or possibly an insult or threat. A legend about the demise of Captain James Cook, the great explorer, illustrates this point.

Legend has it that when Cook arrived in Hawaii, he was observed and met by the understandably curious indigenous people. As he landed and approached them, he put out his hand in what he thought was the universal gesture of friendship, the handshake. The gesture was not as universal as he believed. The group of natives, who had been quite ready to be friendly, interpreted Cook's gesture as threatening and killed him.

Though students in our schools will obviously not go to such extremes, the point is well taken. We must never assume that our interpretation of an action, or lack of action, is the only interpretation possible.

ARTIFACTS

Artifacts refer to the element of nonverbal communication that we consciously create and manipulate. The physical arrangement of classroom furniture is related to this field, which also includes factors such as the colors on the walls, the pictures displayed, the teacher's clothing choices (both the clothes themselves as well as adornments), and how space for different activities or tasks is created. "The clothes make the man" is a saying that may seem passé; nevertheless, what we wear is interpreted by many as a way of defining who we are, the values we represent and the value we place on our interactions with others.

Clothing, mentioned earlier in relation to the blurring of gender lines in the classroom, is a culturally important factor where the teacher is concerned. Though EAL learners and their parents can learn to adjust to casual clothing for their children, a teacher who displays the same casualness is often harder to get used to. In many cultures, the teacher's status implies formality—in speech, relationships and personal presentation, including dress. It may be that parents will find their child's teachers—if clad in runners, jeans and a shirt—a challenge to accept as the competent and well-trained individuals they are. This may be even more so if the teacher is female. Such parents have been known to request a transfer to a more formally dressed teacher's classroom.

In the eyes of immigrants from many cultures, the message sent by a teacher who dresses and speaks casually may be inappropriate. They may believe that teachers who are friendly with students, encourage them to challenge what is said, do not demand that they stand when they speak in class and address them as "sir" or "ma'am," cannot be worthy. If the teacher also dresses quite casually, the negative message is even further reinforced.

In addition, the focal points we choose to set up in our classrooms (reading center, science table, location of the teacher's desk or wherever in the classroom we choose most instruction to take place) speak volumes about our teaching and learning priorities. The time and energy we expend on specific topics of study also reflect what we consider valuable learning and, by inference, what we wish students to value.

SILENCE

Silence has to do with the amount of time our sense of what is comfortable allows for non-talking during communication. This is different from nonverbal behavior which is, of course, not an absence of communication.

The need to fill silence with talk varies greatly among cultural groups. In addition, silence is much more comfortable for relatively longer periods of time with intimates than it is with strangers. In classrooms, silence is demanded for tasks such as silent reading or writing tests, but in personal interactions, such as questioning students, the "wait time" is expected to be very brief.

Some very interesting studies about the wait-time given when carrying on a conversation indicate that, for English speakers, it is relatively short—mere seconds or fractions of seconds. As a result, when interacting with a member of a cultural group used to taking longer to reflect on what to say next, native English speakers virtually prevent this person from getting a word in edgewise. English speakers generally find long silences uncomfortable, and feel compelled to fill them with words.

More will be said on this topic in Chapter Seven, in which the interpretation of silence in conversation is discussed in relation to the values and belief systems that this use of silence can reflect.

TIME

A cherubic seven-year-old enters a corporate boardroom during a meeting. He wishes to give his executive daddy the contents of his piggy bank in return for spending some time with him, because the boy has always heard his father say that, "Time is money."

This excerpt from a television commercial reflects a cultural value that considers time a commodity. Though this may be an extreme case, North American culture does generally treat time in this way.

In many other cultures, by contrast, time is simply the right time to do something—this is the time to eat, the time to marry, the time to plant or the time to harvest. Because the way time is used and the degree of attention paid to it are deeply embedded in cultural values and belief systems, this topic will also be discussed in considerably more detail in Chapter Seven, as well as in the section of the next chapter that deals with attitudes toward schooling.

A Complex Combination

Clearly, communication involves more than simply uttering words. It is worth repeating that the complex elements of coverbal and nonverbal behavior that accompany our words are interrelated, creating communication scenarios that may baffle or please, disturb or reinforce.

The metaphor of the cultural iceberg will be discussed further when we tackle the values and belief systems, symbolically lying submerged, that are the foundational explicit and implicit motivations, the reason and purpose for particular kinds of communication.

Before we move on to this, however, we need to examine another element of who the learners are by becoming aware of the schooling experiences they may or may not bring to our classrooms, and how these impact on their ability to function and interact in our schools. This will be the topic of the next chapter.

Review and Extend

— Think about a situation in which the person to whom you were speaking gave you no feedback at all. How did you feel? What, if anything, did you do? If you have not had such an experience, imagine your reaction and what efforts you could see yourself making to try to engage the listener.

— What coverbal utterances do you make most often? Ask your friends and colleagues. What forms of coverbal utterances do your students make when they are listening to their friends talk?

— We all use gestures to accompany our speech patterns. What gesture do you use to indicate the past? The future? Do your friends use the same gestures as you do?

— When considering proxemics, you may want to think about the following:

  • What is the size of my personal space bubble? Who can invade it, and from whom can I tolerate an infringement of this space? What are the variables that make one level of closeness acceptable and another invasive?

  • How does the closeness of my relationship with someone impact what is acceptable closeness? For

example, consider standing next to a loved one compared to a close friend, an acquaintance or a stranger.
- How do I deal with students or colleagues who invade my space or step on my proxemic toes? Do I talk about it or simply grit my teeth, remove myself from the close contact or wait for the person to move away?

These questions are seldom asked but are worthy of consideration. A measure of self-awareness can go a long way toward preventing miscommunication when, rather than if, such an issue arises.

— When thinking about haptics, here are some questions to consider:
  - Do I allow myself to be touched? By whom? Under what circumstances?
  - Under what conditions would I touch students in my classes and where? Am I sure they understand the purpose and nonverbal meaning of this touch?
  - When meeting parents of students, do I immediately move forward prepared to shake hands regardless of my gender and that of the parent? How would I react if the parent refused to shake my hand?
— Look at the organization of your classroom as though you are seeing it for the first time. What thoughts come to your mind? What does the organization of the room and materials say about you as a teacher and as an individual? Does your desk face the students' desks so that you can observe and supervise them while sitting? Is there room behind your desk for only you, or is another chair close at hand so it can be drawn up for chats with students, colleagues or parents? When you confer with students, do you do it at your desk, or is there a designated spot in the classroom? Does the location allow for side-by-side rather than face-to-face, across-a-barrier contact?
— We all view time through our own cultural biases. What descriptors/adages would you use to identify your view of how we use and manipulate time?

CHAPTER FIVE

EAL LEARNERS AND

SCHOOLING

We must work to create classrooms where there is a discourse
of possibility and hope ... where we are much more attentive to
using the text of students' lives in our work.

Enid Lee

In countries around the world, most schools have
one thing in common: they contain what might be called a
captive audience of learners. Beyond this striking similarity,
however, there are enormous differences among school
systems—in the way they are organized, the way instruction
occurs, and the extent to which they conform with the cultural
norms of a given society. This chapter will identify some of the
difficulties immigrant students and their families experience as
they encounter these differences in a new school, a new country,
and in a new language.

The processes involved in doing school are seldom described
explicitly, and are usually learned over an extended period. No
matter where we were educated, most of us have internalized
our particular experiences of these processes as part of our
concept of attending school. This internalization process began
in early childhood through role-playing and modeling, and
continues throughout the rest of our time in schools, colleges
and universities.

Learning in school is all about communication, and is
therefore also based on culturally different approaches. Ivor
Armstrong Richards, the great educator, noted that successful

communication is always a triumph against odds. What are some common "odds" that we need to consider? Are our learning environments safe and comfortable for *all* our learners? Are they sufficiently quiet to enable learners to hear clearly and attend to each other? Is there an explicit understanding about how words should go together in context to create meaning? Do we reiterate pivotal instructional points over time to ensure our learners "learn" them?

Learning how to do school is an active process that we, as teachers, help children acquire quite deliberately in the early years, but as they grow older we only begin to recognize how deeply rooted our assumptions are when alternative styles of doing school are suddenly presented to us. Zemba, a 13-year-old when he arrived in Canada, is a case in point. Zemba rarely brought the correct books to class and seemed to want to protect all his books. He stood when answering a question, often before the teacher had finished asking it, and used paper very sparingly.

Inviting Zemba to tell about his previous schooling experiences enabled us to understand that these had been very different from the North American experience. For example, he wasn't used to having his own textbooks, as students shared all available print material in his former school. In addition, he was used to classes of 50-60 students, seated two or three to a desk.

In his previous school, students were expected to stand when answering a question, and so he had naturally brought this expectation with him. His haste to answer questions was a learned response to a system in which being recognized as a serious learner by the teacher was extremely important.

Because paper was in very short supply in his former country it was a highly respected commodity that was used sparingly, if at all. As a result, Zemba used only the portion of a single sheet of paper that was absolutely necessary, saving the rest for later use.

Being made aware of these differences provided valuable lessons for all the students, and led to lively discussions about appreciating what we take for granted, respecting property, conservation, and identifying a range of appropriate and inappropriate ways to gain attention.

Zemba's story makes it clear that expectations and behaviors associated with schooling are culture-specific. What students do in one environment may not be easily transferred to, or considered appropriate in, another environment. This is also true of instructional strategies, the topic of the following section.

Instructional Strategies

When planning instructional strategies, we need to consider differences in background and culture. In English-speaking Western countries, teachers tend to use a range of strategies that incorporate large-group discussions, allow for work in pairs or triads, and also focus on cooperative learning and problem-solving activities. Though these strategies are used widely, they are not necessarily familiar to, or even considered appropriate by, others.

Cooperative learning, as a system of instructional strategies, is popular and has many advantages. An inherent assumption of cooperative learning strategies, however, is that the participants have similar beliefs about sharing knowledge. This may not necessarily be so.

In addition, teachers know that learning to work in cooperative groups is not an instantaneous process. Rather it takes considerable time and effort, explicit instruction—and practice—for students to approach learning in this way. If done correctly no one is left out, and all have a learning and participation role to play. Moreover, the group's learning is interdependent—all must do their part for the learning to be successfully accomplished—and all take their responsibility to the group's success quite seriously.

EAL learners from a variety of backgrounds have been taught to act or respond in the classroom in certain ways. As a result, a cooperative learning approach and the concept of sharing knowledge in general may run contrary to all their previous experiences. Sharing may represent a loss of power, influence or privilege, or reflect a loss of competitive spirit. Parents may also view such an approach as an abdication of the responsibility to teach the content. Teachers whose classes include EAL learners need to be aware that all members of the group may not hold the same views on sharing and working together to learn.

In contrast to those who are not used to sharing knowledge, some cultures believe that all knowledge *is* to be shared. Though this level of sharing may epitomize cooperation within a particular cultural milieu, others may view it as undermining motivation to learn, or even call it cheating.

Another factor, related to participation, is the way students have been taught to learn. Some will have learned how to learn by rote and memory, while others will have observed demonstrations without being required to do anything themselves, except watch closely. In still other cultures, students observe until they are ready to do something correctly by themselves.

In many Western cultures, learning by doing is emphasized and trial-and-error is lauded, not censured as in some cultures. While learning style, (also called cognitive style), is rooted in individual predispositions, culture is an overlay that often results in student preferences toward certain approaches.

It is important for teachers to learn about and reflect on the variety of learning systems represented in the classroom. Which students appear to prefer direct instruction that enables them to memorize information, and which seem to be more comfortable employing a trial-and-error approach? Which students blurt out answers or ideas? Which begin to contribute only when they are in smaller groups? On a continuum of approaches to learning, where would each student sit? What do all these variables imply when choosing instructional strategies? Though these questions are intended to help suggest topics for reflection in classrooms that include EAL learners, they are equally valid in monolingual classrooms.

Large-group discussions can help learners identify what they know. In this situation, students who "think with their mouths open"—who blurt out anything that comes to mind—play an important role. While they are jumping in and articulating their responses immediately, they provide time for more hesitant speakers to consolidate what they know or to solidify their knowledge of the English labels associated with the concepts. Individualized attention can be provided when the class is broken into smaller groups, triads or pairs.

Dividing the class into triads, in which each member of the threesome has a specific responsibility, is also a useful way to encourage participation. It provides opportunities for teachers to learn more about a student's language capabilities and to monitor capacity and growth over time.

Group projects are yet another excellent way of involving the additional-language learner. Projects that involve using many different skills give EAL learners an opportunity to participate more fully, demonstrating their range of talents and abilities rather than drowning in a sea of words.

The case of Taki, a nine-year-old girl, illustrates some of the differences and the difficulties caused when a child is required to adapt to a new way of doing things in school. In Taki's former class of 40, the teacher was the transmitter of information, and the students were expected to collectively recite answers to questions. Students were assigned desks, which were arranged in rows facing the front of the room. Rote learning and memorization were common, and students answered questions individually only when the teacher specifically asked.

Taki, like many others, came from an educational system in which the transmission of information was considered far more important than transactions within it. Focusing on the transmission of information occurs for many reasons: large class sizes; few books or supplies; or a belief that this is a better way to teach and learn. This emphasis on acquiring bits of knowledge or facts is very different from the more North American focus on learning how to learn and learning how to gain access to information for a multiplicity of purposes.

Others believe that the process of acquiring information is at least equal in importance to, if not more important than, the end product. Students who are accustomed to one system often have difficulty adjusting to another, and may therefore require specific intervention strategies to help them move from one approach to another.

This was the case with Taki. She needed time and specific instruction to help her identify what was expected of her when working with small groups. Furthermore, she needed her confidence boosted to help her realize that she had contributions to make, as did her peers. While all this was occurring, she was also grappling with the idea that small-group, shared activity was another way of learning.

In summary, focusing on skills and talents rather than language proficiency decreases the pressure to use English in a way that may be beyond their capabilities at this time. Further ideas for working with EAL learners in the classroom are presented in Chapter 8.

Cultural Conflicts

In every situation that includes people from differing cultural backgrounds, there are bound to be clashes between the students' first languages and cultures and those of the host culture. The classroom is no exception.

Students and their families expect what happens in the classroom to reflect their cultural beliefs about education. In North America, for example, play is considered important because of its potential to facilitate learning. In some other cultures, play is considered meaningless and counter-productive to learning. Parents from these cultural backgrounds may become very upset if they see their children playing rather than studying which, in their view, means paper and pencil tasks.

North American classrooms also tend to focus on ideas and creative thinking rather than data-driven learning, which emphasizes memorizing facts. Parents from countries where data-driven learning is the accepted norm sometimes have great difficulty understanding the approaches used in their child's new school world. Differing cultural expectations are exemplified in questions about how a child is doing in school. Some may ask, "Is she happy?" Others may ask, "Is he respectful?" A third group may ask, "Is she doing her best work?" And a fourth may inquire, "Is he neat and tidy?" While a fifth asks, "What is his ranking in the class?" Each of these questions tells us something about the family's values and backgrounds.

Time is an example of an area of potential conflict. The way we conceptualize time and its use is integral to our cultural attitudes. North Americans, for example, tend to view time as a valued commodity, and strive to "make good use of it." The

English language is filled with references to time; it is something to be on, kept, saved, used, spent, lost, gained or even killed. Time spent thinking or daydreaming is often viewed as wasted time or, at least, unproductive time.

People from some other cultural backgrounds neither share nor understand this concept of time. Arriving at school or finishing a task on time can raise questions such as: "Whose time—yours or mine?" "What is so terribly wrong with wanting to take longer to finish the task?"

The identification of school time also reveals differences in perceptions. For some, it is from 9 a.m. to 3 p.m., for others it is from 8 a.m. to 4 p.m. or 7 a.m. to 1 p.m. and may include classes on Saturdays. Some students identify school time as time spent in classes, while others include the time spent in extracurricular activities. How many definitions of school time would your students provide? When working with students, find out how they identify time in their lives outside school, and why this is so. The variety of responses may surprise you. Further discussion of concepts of time is found in Chapter Seven.

A second area of cultural conflict may involve differences in the value accorded the first language as opposed to English. The case of Thi Minh illustrates this.

Thi Minh would speak English in the classroom when called upon, but would revert to Vietnamese on all other occasions. In fact, she seldom spoke and seemed to think that schooling had little to do with her. Her lack of participation in extracurricular activities also concerned her teachers.

With the assistance of another home language speaker, they investigated and found that Thi Minh's family expected her to maintain her traditional language and culture so that she would be able to pass on ancient values and traditions. They believed that acculturation would erode her ability to do this. Further-more, in her village, education was valued for males, but not for females. They also learned that Thi Minh worked after school in her uncle's store and looked after her younger cousins. The demands on her time meant that she could not participate in extracurricular activities.

Developing an awareness of differing cultural values and attitudes helps us understand the factors and forces that shape the lives of our students. It would have been easy for Thi Minh's teachers simply to accept their initial interpretation of her attitudes if they hadn't made the effort to investigate further and learn more about her.

We must understand that we are dealing with a variety of complex and interrelated issues. Adapting to a new society takes time, sometimes even generations. Amending some currently held values (obviously some will never change, nor should they) also takes time.

We must also remember the role played by economics in scenarios such as Thi Minh's. For many immigrants, starting life in a new country often means that the skills, abilities, training and aptitudes they have brought with them are undervalued. In their new country they may be forced to take low-paying and less skilled and responsible jobs than they had previously held. In many families, not only do both parents work, but also both frequently work several jobs in order to survive. For them, this is necessary to lay the foundation for a better life, particularly for their children.

Another factor related to the notion of developing a better life relates to the perception of time discussed earlier. Many families view change and betterment as taking place over several generations or even centuries. North Americans, on the other hand, often have a much greater sense of urgency, and want to see advances within a relatively short period.

A third area of conflict that crops up with great regularity relates to homework, and the expectations that accompany it. For many from Asian cultures, for example, mathematics is the most important part of the curriculum because scores in this subject are critical to determining the rank or standing of a school. As a result, only math homework is considered relevant.

People from many cultural groups expect their children to do more work at home than is frequently the norm in North America. Should insufficient homework be assigned by the teacher, parents have been known to buy workbooks or other materials and insist that students work through them on a daily basis. Often, the students do not fully understand the content of these materials and end up confused and frustrated.

Many parents also expect that homework will be given daily and will start in the earliest school years. By the time students reach secondary school, they are expected to average three to five hours of homework nightly. This facet of student life in Korea is illustrated by the following excerpt from the writing of a young student named Sarah Kang, who is remembering a friend in her home country:

> Her name is Won Hee. She is 18 years old and in Grade 12 in my old school. She wants to be a reporter. She gets up at 6 in the morning. School starts at 7 a.m. We have seven classes a day and extra study time until 10 p.m. After school, she goes to the library to study. She finishes her homework and prepares for the university entrance exam. She goes home at 1 a.m. and eats and then goes to bed. It is her daily life.

> *I'm Not in My Homeland Anymore*
> (edited by Seymour Levitan)

When studying and working hard at school are traits carried over from the home country, what happens to these EAL learners in North America?

During informal conversations, some secondary EAL learners told us that they often spend two to three hours completing homework assignments that might involve one hour's work for a native English speaker. They are checking vocabulary usage, meanings, variations on meanings and spelling, and doing other reference work. Some have quietly added that to get to bed before 2 a.m. is a luxury. The opposite extreme might be a child who quickly sees he is far ahead in some subject areas and responds by not doing any work at all. The lack of pressure makes it easy to assume school here is inferior.

A fourth area of conflict relates to the choices students are asked to make. In many elementary classrooms, for example, learning activities are organized in modules or stations, where students choose their own starting points. In secondary schools, students' choices may relate to selecting optional or elective courses.

Students coming from some other educational systems have often had little or no experience with making choices like these. They are accustomed to having all their courses prescribed, with rigidly articulated performance expectations. Asking a student to choose a starting point, or one course over another, may generate questions such as: "How do I decide?" "How do I know what's more or less important?" "What if I choose wrong?" "How do these courses relate to anything else?" "How much time do I spend on each?" "Will I get an A on my report card?" When even English-speaking students sometimes find it difficult to make these decisions, just imagine how difficult it must be for some EAL learners!

Understanding the dilemmas that we may be creating, even inadvertently, for EAL students is important. Sometimes, we may need to identify strategies that limit the range of choices for these students, at least until they feel more comfortable with the process. It is also useful to have a bilingual speaker available to explain procedures and your teaching style to the students and their families in their first language. Additional questions and concerns can also be dealt with directly at this time.

Inviting parents to come to the school to do this, however, raises another area of potential cultural dissonance. In many countries in the world parents have no involvement with the schools, nor is there any expectation that they *will* be involved. In fact, parents are often asked to come to the school only when there is a serious problem. This doesn't mean, however, that there isn't support for teachers—quite the contrary! There is solid support for them, but it is expressed in different ways.

In some cultures, the teacher's word is law. This often means that parents don't believe they have the right to question or "interfere with" what goes on at school; difficulties are considered the student's responsibility and are frequently interpreted as a failure to try hard enough.

In other cultures, parents show their respect for teachers by giving them full and supported authority to do as they see fit. This often includes approval to discipline the student physically. A failure to do homework, for example, might result in a caning from the teacher. At home, parents are likely to add their own corporal punishment to further support this action. The fact that corporal punishment is not condoned in North American schools may therefore come as a surprise to some parents and should, as a result, be carefully explained to all parents.

Views about the relationship between school and home are often very different from those that prevail in North America, where parents are considered partners in the education of their children. While this view is desirable and supported by research, it is often extremely difficult for families from some cultural groups to embrace because of differences in cultural conditioning and experiences. It may take a long time before they are comfortable participating at a level that is customary in North America.

To introduce and facilitate parental involvement, teachers may wish to consider providing information sessions in the students' first languages. It may also be helpful to identify community leaders who are prepared to function as networking coordinators for other community members. It's always pleasantly astonishing to discover just how many people, when they are asked, are prepared to assist with solving settlement problems for newcomers.

Building Bridges

What do these difficulties and differences mean? They mean that we, as educators, must heighten our level of awareness and recognize that differences exist. We must also continually probe and question, and never assume anything, as we work to increase our understanding of the various backgrounds the students bring to our classrooms. Although we may have no difficulty acknowledging that the world is shrinking, we need to further our understanding of the implications of this for the day-to-day work in our classrooms.

We also have a responsibility to look beyond the obvious difficulties and differences, and try to seek out the similarities. We must strive to identify areas of cross-cultural commonality in order to build bridges for and with EAL learners and their families. These bridges will help us—and the students—adjust to the new realities in which we all find ourselves.

Even with the need to continually build bridges we have learned, over time, that some EAL learners arrive with particular additional learning needs. The needs of three groups of such learners are the topic of the next chapter.

Review and Extend

— When welcoming learners from other countries, it is helpful to know something about the education system from which they have come. Get material from a library, or research an education system in a country about which you know little. Compare it with the education system in which you teach.

— Imagine a school in a developing country where resources are very scarce. Describe it to a friend or colleague, and together consider how you would teach in that situation.

— Think about your own personal philosophy of learning. What are the important components in it? If you put process or product on a scale of importance, where would each one sit? How might the positions vary with differing academic disciplines?

— We all have a preferred learning style, such as visual, auditory, kinesthetic. What are the preferred learning styles of your students? How has this awareness impacted your teaching?

— Make a list of as many possible things you can do with time, such as save time, kill time, waste time, and so on. See if you can find out what expressions members of other cultures use to refer to time.

CHAPTER SIX

LEARNING AND LITERACY FOR "SPECIAL" EAL LEARNERS

Every child is gifted.
They just unwrap their packages at different times.

Anon.

EAL learners bring with them a range of skills and strengths and an intact oral communication system in their first language. What they do not have are strong English language skills. We must make sure that we remember what they *do* have, and not always focus on their weaknesses, namely a lack of English.

Many new arrivals, depending on their age at arrival, will be able to cope with North American schooling systems with varying degrees of success. They will be able to use their knowledge of how to do school, be familiar with school routines and expectations, and be able to utilize their own learning strategies in their new situations.

Other learners, however, will have more difficulty with schooling. Teachers need to become aware of who these learners are, and what needs to be understood about them and their learning needs in relation to the structure and organization of North American schooling systems.

For the purposes of this book, "special" EAL learners include the following broadly termed categories:

- — EAL learners who arrive as refugees
- — EAL learners with additional learning needs
- — EAL learners who exhibit elements of giftedness

Considerations

Before considering these groups of learners in greater detail, there are several points about schooling and learning that are particularly relevant to the needs of these types of learners.

The first consideration is the definition of success that is used most frequently by many school systems. In reality, many systems use:

- — Letter grades
- — Graduation rates
- — Course stream (academic v. non-academic/vocational)
- — Percentage marks on provincial/state exams
- — Eligibility for university enrolment
- — Awards and scholarships
- — Standardized test scores

These are all *quantatively* based measurements that pertain to academic success. Many school systems tend to make parents and learners feel that academic success is the only benchmark worthy of attainment. Indeed, many parents in a variety of countries also believe that academic success is the only laudable standard. The learners identified above may be achieving success in school, but their success needs to be identified by other criteria.

For example, refugee learners who have had limited schooling, interrupted schooling, or no schooling at all prior to their arrival, may not be able, in the short term, to meet the above criteria for academic success. This should not mean, though, that they are not successful. Alternative definitions of what constitutes success are offered later in this chapter.

The second point to consider relates to the extensive use of the term "literacy." In many instances, the term is used in schools but there isn't necessarily a common, shared definition of it, even among members of one school staff. We used to think that literacy meant the ability to learn to read and write. Lee Gunderson, in his book, *English Only Instruction and Immigrant Students in Secondary Schools: A Critical Examination*, (2007), (page 11) reported that:

> Teachers generally appear to hold the view that teaching literacy skills is central to their mission—that literacy is the basic foundation of learning. They are often convinced that their most important role is to develop independent critical thinkers. They appear to hold a view of learning, an extremely complex model of language learning, that is literacy-centered, that views reading and writing as integral activities of thinking human beings designed to produce independent critical thinkers. These are fairly well-ingrained North American views not necessarily shared by individuals from other cultures.

It is increasingly clear that literacy encompasses a much more complex and much broader concept. In 2008, the National Council of Teachers of English (NCTE) adopted a statement of 21st century literacies as the need to:

— Develop proficiency with the tools of technology.
— Build relationships with others to pose and solve problems collaboratively and cross-culturally.
— Design and share information for global communities to meet a variety of purposes.
— Manage, analyze and synthesize multiple streams of simultaneous information.
   Create, critique, analyze and evaluate multi-media texts.
— Attend to the ethical responsibilities required by these complex environments.

What is inherent throughout all of the above is the idea that literacy has always been a collection of cultural and communicative practices shared among members of particular groups.

A third consideration is that it is important to remember the difference between communicative language and academic language. Decades ago, Jim Cummins of the Ontario Institute for Studies in Education coined the terms BICS (basic interpersonal communicative skills) and CALP (cognitive academic language proficiency) to differentiate between these two general language-related skill sets.

BICS refers to the conversational, social, everyday language of learners. It is language in a context-rich setting and fluency can take between one and three years to acquire. This stage may also include a "silent" period in which learning does not appear to be taking place. However, students *are* learning. They are processing the language, and will feel ready to participate in due course.

Teachers have reported silent periods lasting more than a year, but usually students are eager to communicate well before then. Because of our expectations for communication in the classroom, we tend to feel very uncomfortable with an extended period of silence from a learner. It is important not to jump to conclusions about that learner's cognitive ability simply because they have chosen to process their initial learning in this way.

CALP is the language of academia and textbooks. It takes a minimum of five years to develop an intermediate fluency, and a lifetime to develop CALP fully. Unlike BICS, where the majority of the words used have common Anglo-Saxon roots, CALP language is increasingly formal. CALP moves to French, Latin and Greek rooted words that are not part of everyday conversation but are the core of what makes language sound adult and professional.

For example, consider your conversation with someone after you have served on jury duty. In conversation you would be relating what was being *asked* and answered and that the trial was now *over*. In a more formal setting or a textbook, it is likely reference would be made to *questioning* and *interrogation* and the trial would be *concluded*. These differences are often not made explicit for learners and, as a result, many EAL learners start working in textbooks and think they are starting over as they try to grasp what they are reading—the text seems to be filled with totally new vocabulary.

Cummins' research has been replicated repeatedly, confirming his "length of time" findings. Consider then, if BICS and CALP were presented as an iceberg, BICS would be the small upper part of the iceberg that can be seen, while CALP remains that massive language component hidden below the surface of the water. As we turn our attention to our three categories of special learners, let's consider how much more the challenges outlined above—how we define success, literacy and language proficiency—are likely to impact their learning efforts.

EAL Learners Who Arrive as Refugees

> **Geneva Convention Definition of a Refugee (1951, 1967)**
>
> *A refugee is a person who "owing to (a) well-founded fear of being persecuted for reasons of race, religion, nationality, membership of a particular social group or political opinion, is outside the country of his nationality and is unable or, owing to such fear, is unwilling to avail himself of the protection of the country; or who, not having a nationality and being outside the country of his former habitual residence ..., is unable or, owing to such fear, is unwilling to return to it."*
>
> UNHCR, 2007

A number of refugees are arriving in the English-speaking world from countries in which they had no opportunity to attend school. This may be because they were born in a refugee camp where there were no schools. In some camps, however, where an education system did exist, the class size may have been astronomical compared with what we take for granted here.

Others may have come from mountainous or desert terrain where schools simply did not exist. Their efforts, before arriving, would have been focused on developing survival skills, and learning in the schooling sense would include orally learning traditional components of their culture.

Still others may have been denied learning opportunities because of their social status, religious belief systems, gender, or because they were part of a group being persecuted by the current government of their country.

Part of the difficulty teachers have is to identify who the EAL refugee learners are. They don't arrive with overt signs of their status, so we need to find out as much background information from their documents as possible, and observe how they function in class. Since it is likely there is minimal information available about any schooling experiences they may have had, observation is a key way to learn what they can and cannot yet manage in a classroom setting.

Some of the arriving refugees are in their teens. They may have good oral communication skills in their home languages, but have had no access to learning the written form, if one exists. In the book, *Closing the Achievement Gap* (2002) by Yvonne Freeman et al., the authors identify on page 33 certain shared characteristics, particularly for teen refugees:

— They are over age for their grade-level placement due to their weak academic skills or inadequate formal schooling.
— They have needs that traditional EAL and bilingual programs, and regular programs for English speakers, cannot or do not meet.
— They have no or low literacy skills in their first language or in English, and have little academic content-area knowledge.
— They are socially and psychologically isolated from mainstream students.
— They need approaches and materials that will help them catch up to and compete with mainstream students.
— They are at risk of failing or dropping out in traditional academic programs.

For EAL refugee teens in particular, we must be ever mindful of the extensive differences between their backgrounds and their new learning environments. For some, they will have neither the time nor the inclination to acquire "academic" language, even though they attend school regularly. Family financial survival is their first priority. Others, despite all their best efforts, will have insufficient time to meet academic graduation criteria within the timeframes allowed by current schooling systems.

In thinking about alternative criteria to identify their success in school, several examples, generated in part by a group of these learners themselves, include the following advice to newcomers:

— Attend regularly
— Do homework
— Finish projects
— Help other students
— Ask the teacher for help
— Respect the teacher
— Follow the school's code of conduct
— Find a place of belonging
— Be engaged in the class work

The previous facets of success can be viewed as equally valid. Rather than "academics first," emphasis needs to be placed on assisting refugee teen learners to:

— Acquire as much functional/BICS language as possible.
— Utilize primarily hands on approaches (where safety factors allow) to demonstrate learners' skill development and understandings.
— Work with a partner or in a small group as much as possible.

Since these learners and their families will probably have a focus on getting a job as quickly as possible, having some basic communication skills combined with experience in working with others will be of great benefit towards realizing this goal. Providing these learners with what is termed "functional literacy" may therefore prove to be an optimal first step. (The term functional literacy is used to describe reading and writing skills that are adequate to cope with the demands of everyday life in a complex society, and incorporates reading materials that relate directly to community development and to teaching relevant life and work skills.)

While these may be practical realities for the majority of EAL refugee teens, there will always be exceptions. We are familiar with instances in which EAL refugee learners started school in a sheltered EAL class, and within one year were functioning well at their appropriate grade levels. The point is not to have lower expectations for any teenage refugee learner. Instead we must continually assess their progress, listen as much and as closely as possible to their wants and needs in terms of the learning they most desire, and allow for multiple opportunities for them to work with others. In time, all of these experiences will empower them to make the best possible decisions.

As a footnote, since becoming involved with EAL learners, and most particularly refugees, we ourselves have continuously learned more about geography and global "hot spots" than we could ever have imagined. Learning from your learners, sometimes as much as they learn from you, is what makes teaching such an endlessly fascinating profession.

EAL Learners with Additional Learning Needs

Students who have difficulties learning, for example those who are EAL students and are learning disabled, may not be able to meet the usual criteria of academic success. We need to ensure, however, that their progress is supported appropriately. It is important to note that, for learners coming from many countries, there may be no concept or language for "learning disability." Because there is no equivalent for many learning disability terms, we cannot presume understanding of them, or their educational implications, by either the parents or by the learners themselves.

In fact, many parents will deny that their children have any difficulty with learning. A common response to teachers is, "He'll just have to work harder, or longer hours." It often takes considerable time, effort and patience before teachers and parents are on the same page regarding how best to support a learner's slower or more challenging progress.

One of the conundrums for teachers who work with EAL learners is attempting to determine:

— What progress is, or is not, being made.
— Why the student is not progressing.
— If the problem is language or learning.

First it must be recognized that, if an EAL learner has not had the kind of home literacy environment our school systems consider the norm, it would be easy to assume that there is something wrong. Snap judgments such as an impoverished environment and/or lack of preparation for school come all too readily to mind. However, what is really at play here may in fact be a completely different way of living and learning.

For example, a child from a country where school does not begin until the age of seven would arrive here, be put in a Grade 2 class and certainly appear to be significantly behind. When you consider how much a child learns in those first two school years, the response from a teacher might well be to assume that there is a learning problem. If the learner happens to be of secondary school age and does not appear to have the prerequisite doing school skills needed to begin learning in a new language, this gap is then much wider still. Interestingly enough we tend to make more accommodation for a teen without previous schooling than for a child in the early years of schooling. The belief that "children just soak up language" is at play here, and must be re-examined with new eyes and in the light of new evidence.

Second, it is important to remember that all learners new to a language, its culture, and its schooling system will experience some forms of culture shock, as outlined in Chapter One. Culture shock, in extreme cases, has been known to last for months, even years. Though we cannot make an assumption that a child who does not thrive in school is simply in culture shock, it is a factor to consider when progress appears to be slow.

Cultural differences can mean the learner is reluctant to speak, will seem extremely passive, or will refuse to participate in some activities with peers of the opposite sex. Finally, linguistic differences can mean the learner has pronunciation difficulties. For example, the learner may find some English language sounds difficult to imitate, or in some cases will simply not hear the sound you are trying to help her/him learn.

Keeping the above in mind as mitigating factors, the list that follows includes some of the more obvious assumptions we make about what learners understand/know/bring to school:

- Reading/writing progresses left to right/top to bottom.
- Roman alphabet system.
- Sound/symbol relationships.
- Beginning, middle, end is the "right" order of events in storytelling.
- Holding a pen/pencil in a "proper" grip.
- Raising a hand to have a speaking turn in class.
- Using a pencil sharpener.
- Playground/gym turn taking.
- Borrowing and returning school/personal property.
- Being on time.
- Taking turns talking.
- Using a locker, and knowing how a combination lock works.
- Students change classes (rather than the teacher) and do not get lost.
- Participation in all activities is normal and expected.
- Learning by trial and error is what "everyone" does.

The process for beginning to address these assumptions takes time, and involves multiple steps. Some of the things we can do/ask include:

- Start by considering the possibility that the difficulties may have a physical origin. Have the child's hearing and vision checked. The hearing check should be a proper audiological one, not a "tuning fork" test. The vision checks should include a 12" (30 cm) test and a 20' (6 m) test. These reflect reading/book distance, and the typical distance between the child and the board.
- Learn as much as possible about the child's previous developmental history and schooling, such as the age at which the child walked and talked, the age when the child first started school, the existence of any learning difficulties in the first language. You may want to talk with an Early Childhood Education specialist or a medical professional about childhood developmental norms.
- Give yourself and the learner a significant amount of time (several months) to see if apparent problems persist.

— Review copies of the student's output, for example, that involve numbers and print/written material, to see if errors are consistent or haphazard. EAL learners generally make consistent errors; learning-disabled learners generally make inconsistent ones.
— Gather information over time.
— Document your efforts about trying a variety of instructional strategies, and identify those that seem to work best.
— Assess in the student's home language, if appropriate, or with nonverbal instruments. It should be noted that nonverbal instruments are every bit as culturally biased as those that are written text in a "foreign-to-the-child" language and should, therefore, be used with extreme caution.

While the focus so far has been on EAL learners who may have some kind of learning disability or lack of schooling experience, we must also recognize that there may be learners who have more complex learning needs.

It is reasonable to think that most cultural groups throughout the world probably have the same percentage of children with more complex learning needs as those statistically found in North American populations. Thus an EAL learner may also be a Down's syndrome child, or be on the autistic spectrum, or have cerebral palsy. These children need a team of trained specialists working with the classroom teacher and school staff to provide appropriate instructional strategies and support.

EAL Learners Who Exhibit Elements of Giftedness

Researchers postulate that about two percent of any given population is gifted. While school systems throughout North America, Britain and Australia have created mechanisms for identifying gifted learners, and providing a variety of levels of support for them, this is not necessarily the norm in many other countries.

It is often difficult to identify gifted learners when they speak the language of the community. It is even more difficult to identify such learners when they do not have English as a home language, or when they are in the process of learning it. Some of the barriers faced by EAL learners when they first enter school include:

— An environment that is unlike any in their previous experience.
— A disconnect between home and life outside the home.
— A curriculum that seems irrelevant to their lives.
— Instruction that is not deemed to be relevant to their needs.
— A sense of alienation.
— An assumption that because they are limited in English proficiency, they are less able.

All of these factors impinge upon performance, let alone on one's best performance.

DEFINITION OF GIFTED

There are many definitions of gifted and talented learners. Two definitions we find appealing are:

The term "gifted and talented" when used in respect to students, children or youth means students, children or youth who give evidence of high performance capability in areas such as intellectual, creative, artistic, or leadership capacity, or in specific academic fields, and who require services or activities not ordinarily provided by the school in order to fully develop such capabilities.

(NCLB: Title IX, Part A, Section 9101(22), p. 544)

The majority of states in the United States have adopted this definition, completely or in part. For example, a slightly different definition has been developed and used in the state of Texas. This definition reads:

(The phrase) "gifted and talented student" means a child or youth who performs at or shows potential for performing at a remarkably high level of accomplishment when compared to others of the same age, experience, or environment, and who exhibits high performance capability in an intellectual, creative or artistic area; possesses an unusual capacity for leadership; or excels in a specific academic field.

(74th Legislature of the State of Texas, Chapter 29,
Subchapter D, Section 29.121)

These definitions have the following major characteristics:

— Diversity of areas in which performance may be exhibited, for example intellectual, creative, artistic, leadership, academic.
— Comparison with other groups, such as those in general education classrooms or of the same age, experience, or socio-economic environment.
— Use of terms that imply a need for services and activities not normally provided by the school in order to develop the capability and potential of the learner's gift(s).

These definitions also move away from previously held views that giftedness could be measured by an IQ test and/or standardized test score. An increasing number of educators are looking to identify the "able learner" rather than the more narrowly defined gifted student who scores in the top three per cent on IQ tests.

How does any definition relate to those learners who do not have English as their home language? The identification and assessment of gifted and talented EAL learners is complex and challenging. When we move into this arena, we must acknowledge that many of us may have preconceived biases which hinder opportunities for appropriate identification of these learners.

There are several challenges facing us when it comes to identifying and providing appropriate educational services to EAL gifted learners. Carole Harris in 1993 in *Identifying and Serving Recent Immigrant Children Who Are Gifted* identified a number of these:

— *Linguistic.* The process of additional language learning is long, complex and developmental. Therefore, using

English-based assessment instruments can lead to erroneous conclusions.

— *Cultural*. Traditional customs, gender-specific behaviors, differences in learning styles and response patterns can lead to misinterpreted messages.
— *Economic*. Recent arrivals may be poorer than in their countries of origin as they are often sending money "home" to support families or extended families.
— *Attitudinal*. Immigrants may look favorably upon schools/schooling, while simultaneously having guilt feelings about family members who were left behind, or whose whereabouts are unknown.
— *Socio-Cultural and Peer Expectations*. Ethnic or racial conflict, concern for personal safety, or conflicting peer expectations may cause tension and interfere with performance.
— *Cross-Cultural*. Cross-cultural content is confusing and frequently stressful for learners, who find that their stress is often difficult to articulate.
— *Intergenerational*. Immigrant students often act as "interpreters" for the family, regardless of their fluency in English. Heightened levels of stress can make some learners withdraw from participating in activities, thus making it difficult to assess their abilities.
— *School Placement*. A small number of students may arrive with incorrect information about their ages because accurate records were not available, or because the way a child's age is recorded differs.

These challenges mean we need to be more aware of, and sensitive to, differing nuances that may suggest areas of potential strengths.

Here are some examples of EAL students we have encountered who evidenced aspects of "giftedness:"

— While on a field study to nearby botanical gardens, an elementary learner from a war-torn country announced that he could do 50 different things with a piece of bamboo.

— A secondary-aged refugee learner was of slight stature; however he excelled in wrestling, and is now on a university wrestling team.
— A severely learning disabled elementary learner had difficulty with all aspects of the curriculum, yet demonstrated outstanding fashion design ability.
— A teen learner could orate and engage in discussions with an extremely high degree of verbal fluency, but could not put these same thoughts/arguments on paper.
— A teen refugee learner could hear a piece of music twice, and then play it through, accurately, on a piano.

Some commonly used techniques for identifying gifted EAL learners include:

— Multiple assessment measures to give students several opportunities to demonstrate their skills and performance potential.
— Assessment in a student's home language.
— Behavioral checklists, inventories or nominations.
— Interviews, self-reports, autobiographies, and case histories.

The most important facet of these techniques is to provide a range of opportunities, over time, for EAL learners to demonstrate their competence, or growing competence, in an area. Teachers are often the first to notice unusual performance in certain areas. Keeping notes over time to see what the true picture of such a learner may be can be very helpful at a later, more formal identification stage.

One of the things that teachers frequently find is that some parents will inform their child's teacher that their child is gifted, implying that this is so in all areas of life. A number of parents think that this label will somehow raise their social status, particularly in a new community where so many things are different. And, indeed, the child may have very good abilities in one or more areas, but this could also be the result of extra time spent focusing on these selected areas. This is a good reason for you to ensure that a learner's purported abilities are explored over time.

Other parents do not wish their child to be labeled in any way, including gifted. One concern may be that their child will be separated from friends. Another is that they are aware of the differences between the child's ability in specific areas and the child's social/emotional development. An additional concern may relate to the child's personality and his/her perceived need to be outstanding at all times.

Working with a variety of EAL learners enables us, as teachers, to continually grow and hone our own skills. The more proficient we become, the better able we are to work more effectively with all our learners.

Reference has been made in this chapter to the influences that culture has on our learners. This moves us into the arena of values and belief systems. Values and beliefs underlie all aspects of culture and communication, and an appreciation for and understanding of how they can affect what happens in given contexts will greatly enhance our ability to work with learners from many cultures. We shall be discussing values and beliefs in the next chapter.

Review and Extend

—   In your classroom and with your students, consider the number of different definitions of "success" you use.
—   Discuss the term "literacy" with colleagues. How similar is the thinking among you?
—   Borrow books or media about refugee experiences from friends or the local library. Some examples of books are:
    •   *A Long Walk to Water* (Linda Sue Park)
    •   *Bullets on the Water*: *Refugee Stories* (compiled and edited by Ivaylo Grouev)
    •   *I Live Here* (Mia Kirshner; J.B. McKinnon; Paul Shoebridges; Michael Simons)
    •   *Left to Tell*: *Discovering God Amidst the Rwandan Holocaust* (Immaculée Ilibagiza)
    •   *Shattered*: *Stories of Children and War* (edited by Jennifer Armstrong)
    •   *The Bite of the Mango* (Mariatu Kamara)

- *The Lost Boys Of Sudan: An American Story of the Refugee Experience* (Mark Bixler)
- *To Destroy You Is No Loss: The Odyssey of a Cambodian Family* (JoAnn D. Criddle and Teeda Butt Mam)

Some examples of DVDs are:
- *Don't Fence Me In: Major Mary and the Karen Refugees from Burma* (a film by Ruth Gumnit)
- *God Grew Tired of Us* (produced by Brad Pitt and narrated by Nicole Kidman)
- *Strangers No More* (directed by Karen Goodman and Kirk Simon)
— Review the list of assumptions about what learners understand/know/bring to school. Think of additional assumptions and add them to the list.
— Start making a list of local and other resources that you may want to access to meet EAL learner needs.

. . . .

CHAPTER SEVEN

VALUES AND BELIEFS

The belief that one's own view of reality is the only reality,
is the most dangerous of all delusions.

Paul Watzlawick

So far our discussion has focused on a number of aspects of communication, culture and the individual circumstances that influence the actions and interactions of the students with whom we work. In this chapter, we will examine more closely the underlying values and belief systems that, translated into action or inaction, often lie at the root of miscommunication. But before examining this foundation in detail, a visual representation of all we have touched on so far (and what is yet to come) seems appropriate. Else Hamayan, prolific author and noted educator, conceived a version of the cultural iceberg as illustrated in this diagram. You will note many details we have already discussed, and possibly see examples you may not yet have considered.

While we deliberately draw rather black and white portraits for illustrative purposes, it must be understood that interactions and motivations are far more complex. For example, when considering the following dichotomies and then simply adding an age to the individuals being portrayed, everything changes. Taking the example of a young child being defiant or submissive evokes one image, while the same being told of a teenager immediately sparks a number of other possibilities to do with

What is Culture?

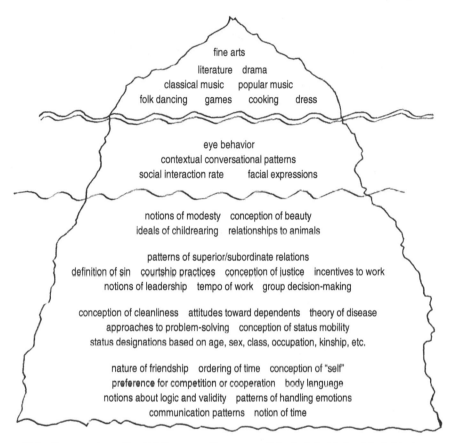

fine arts

literature   drama

classical music   popular music

folk dancing   games   cooking   dress

eye behavior

contextual conversational patterns

social interaction rate   facial expressions

notions of modesty   conception of beauty

ideals of childrearing   relationships to animals

patterns of superior/subordinate relations

definition of sin   courtship practices   conception of justice   incentives to work

notions of leadership   tempo of work   group decision-making

conception of cleanliness   attitudes toward dependents   theory of disease

approaches to problem-solving   conception of status mobility

status designations based on age, sex, class, occupation, kinship, etc.

nature of friendship   ordering of time   conception of "self"

preference for competition or cooperation   body language

notions about logic and validity   patterns of handling emotions

communication patterns   notion of time

the growing up struggles that characterize actions and interactions during the teen years.

Gender and the sense of being part of a group also play significant roles when considering values and belief systems from a teen standpoint, but it is not specifically included in the five continua we present on the following pages. While gender is an overarching factor to be considered, the continua represent polar opposites in an effort to highlight the complexities that underpin classroom interactions.

These continua are by no means the only versions that have been postulated and discussed across the world. Aside from the two frameworks already noted, that of Robert Kohls' on page 28 and Geert Hofstede's on page 29, several others have been created, some with more, some with fewer, variables across a range of dimensions. As Sachiyo Shearman noted in the paper she presented at the International Communication Association Conference in 2008, these frameworks/continua "... share some basic assumptions in conceptualization and methodological approach, yet ... provide us with a unique understanding of the universal human values structures."

The research and popular literature on cross-cultural communication abounds with examples of apparently inexplicable communication breakdowns. It also clearly highlights how differences in values and belief systems can affect all aspects of communication. Values and beliefs constitute the base of the cultural iceberg, the foundation upon which rest all the previously discussed elements of communication and culture.

In *Beyond Culture*, Edward T. Hall pointed out that "... there is not one aspect of human life that is not touched and altered by culture" (page 16). Though there is tacit agreement about the truth of this statement, the depth of meaning in these simple words is often seriously underestimated. It relates to the kinds of underlying cultural values and belief systems that sometimes spark people to wonder how anyone could possibly "act that way."

We all have a basic set of principles that guide how we live, how we interact with others, and those with whom we choose to associate. Within a given cultural group, these principles are often not articulated into a clear focus or creed.

Instead, this underlying set of principles is rather like the control system necessary to run a subway. No one riding the subway really notices or is consciously aware of it—until the subway breaks down. This is an apt metaphor for what happens when intercultural interactions go wrong.

Because our underlying values and belief systems guide much of our approach to daily life, recognizing and understanding them is very important to teachers when working with EAL learners. It is in this area, however, that it is often hardest to step outside oneself and reach out to others because, in attempting to do this, we are trying to override the mostly unconscious patterns that regulate how we live our lives.

All cultural groups have values and belief systems. As noted, many elements of these systems are shared; but many are not—and it is in these latter areas that the roots of conflict reside. When one's cultural toes are trodden upon, it rankles and affects communication long after any specific incident that could be talked about and dealt with on the spot.

Rather than reacting angrily to or ignoring differences that cause friction, developing some insight into and understanding of the key elements that make up culture at this unconscious level can be helpful. As teachers, the onus is on us, the adults, to step back and take the larger view, consider the underlying motivators that have brought about the misunderstanding, and act appropriately in the best interests of the students. When we do this, our increased level of understanding will prove a balm for our poor bruised toes.

In this chapter, we will use several global constructs to address a number of the cultural motivators that can lead to misunderstandings. These constructs are presented as opposites that can be visualized as two ends of a continuum. Recognizing where we sit on each continuum, particularly in relation to students, helps us understand and gain insights into our responses when a particular position seems to be challenged by a communication breakdown. It will also help us move forward and take the actions necessary to resolve the miscommunication.

If you have not already done so, we suggest that you think about and decide where you fit on the continua introduced in Chapter Two. Going through the same exercise as you read this chapter will likely be an enlightening experience. Knowing your own comfort level will enable you to deal more effectively with learners who are at different points on each continuum.

Assertiveness—Compliance

In North American English-speaking cultures, we tend to believe in the power of self-help—the ability to make something of ourselves if only we make an effort and work hard. In other words, we are inclined to believe that we control all the practical aspects of our own fate. Exceptions might be made in cases where there is a genetic handicap or physical disability, though many would deem that these, too, should be wrestled into relative submission.

This basic belief has diverse and immensely complex consequences. It enables us to dismiss and even condemn those who don't thrive, those who are forced to turn to various forms of social assistance or, worse yet, to opt out emotionally by using addictive substances. It also enables many of us to ignore the broken individuals who sleep in parks, stand in lines at soup kitchens or beg at the doors of the stores where those who have "made it" spend their surplus cash.

In fact, some people are even suspicious of the growing numbers on social assistance rolls and of those who go for help to the ever-increasing numbers of food banks. We harbor a nagging belief that if only they had worked harder and spent a little more wisely, they would not find themselves in such a predicament.

Contrast this belief with the attitudes and actions that might be generated by a conviction that our role in society is preordained from birth, and that all that befalls us in life is part and parcel of our inevitable fate while on this earth. If we are born to wealth and status, this is both a birthright and a responsibility. If we are born into desperate poverty this, too, is as it should be, and efforts to change this reality are looked upon as futile.

Though there are certainly those who view the universe unfolding from the perspective of one of these two extremes—fate versus individual control—most people would locate themselves somewhere in between. Our position on the continuum influences many of our actions and interactions with others.

Our notion of the desirability of standing up for ourselves, for example, is influenced by this position. Standing up for ourselves implies asserting our rights as individual human beings in any context. English-speaking cultures have a variety of negative metaphors—being a pushover or a doormat—to describe those who do not act in accordance with this belief.

"The squeaky wheel gets the grease" is a cliché often used to justify self-assertive behavior. Yet, in some cultures, "the nail that sticks up is hammered down" is considered a more appropriate metaphor. When cooperation and consensus building are of greatest value, asserting individual needs is considered highly inappropriate because it undermines the harmony of the group.

In North American English-speaking classrooms, we usually try to balance the need to keep some sense of order with our efforts to create a relatively democratic atmosphere in which individuals can assert themselves. "Groupthink," where everyone is expected to react in unison and act as a collective whole without considering individual needs, is viewed unfavorably in many English-speaking contexts.

Consider how students who have been trained from infancy not to stand out as individuals are likely to react in this setting. They are likely to suffer at the hands of their peers—and teachers—without protest, and become distressed when asked to express their own opinions. Often they literally do not have an opinion until the teacher gives them one. A related issue is the case of students with obvious artistic talent who have been "programmed" from birth to become doctors or lawyers, ignoring anything that might make them stray from their predetermined paths.

As teachers, we may find it frustrating to deal with these students and hard to understand their passive attitudes. It is very easy for us to judge them deficient in some way because, we reason, if they were able to think clearly, then surely they would be able to express their own thoughts. Alternatively, we might just as easily think ill of their "overbearing" parents who allow their children so little freedom and individuality.

Furthermore, innate differences in temperament, rather than culture, sometimes incur the same feelings of confusion and frustration. An idealist dealing with someone who is very practical, or a spiritually oriented person dealing with a materialistic, acquisitive type—and *vice versa*—may experience the same feelings.

Finally, the assertiveness-compliance continuum also includes our beliefs about the value of change. North American English-speaking cultures tend to view change as positive, a chance to flex metaphorical muscles, grow and learn in a process that can be frightening, but also exciting. This contrasts sharply with a culture in which deeply embedded, centuries-old traditions are the supreme values.

We continue to receive into our classrooms many refugee and, in some cases, immigrant children whose sense of stability, continuity and reliance on traditional ways of life have been seriously disrupted. In many cases, they are unlikely to view change for its own sake in the same positive light that we do.

In fact, children raised in English-speaking cultures sometimes resist and resent change but usually, in remarkably short order, they become excited about new possibilities if they are presented in positive and inviting terms. This positive attitude is the basis of our belief system that change is almost universally for the better.

Dominance—Submission

The assertiveness-compliance continuum focuses on the power of the individual to effect change, and relates to individual traits and beliefs about innate power with which we may or may not be endowed. Aside from individual, personal biases, culture is considered the major determining factor in deciding where on this continuum individuals feel comfortable. Firmly linked to the relative power of the individual, however, is the role of the individual in his or her cultural group.

This is, in essence, the power dimension examined by Hofstede and referred to in an earlier chapter. The various roles and relationships that are part of existence in a social-cultural group determine where each of us sits on the dominance-submission continuum. In fact, our relative position is often redefined with each separate role we play and how we are involved in various working and personal relationships.

Our most basic roles and attendant relationships relate to gender. The way a culture defines male and female roles has major implications for us in the classroom. As indicated earlier,

94

a student's gender can affect attendance and class participation, as well as personal choices or perceived options. Chapter Five highlighted some of these issues, including attitudes toward education that depend on a variety of factors, including the gender of the students.

In English-speaking cultures, we have become increasingly ambivalent about how carefully we attend to gender differences. On the one hand, we endorse unisex clothing and hairstyles, while on the other we set distinctly different standards for girls than for their male peers, especially once they pass puberty. Feminism began as a movement toward the emancipation of, and equal rights for, women, and is now sometimes branded as un-female by groups that advocate traditional family lifestyles, where the mother is the homemaker and raises the children while the father goes out to work. We are bombarded with images of provocatively clad stars of music videos, and witness variations on their "stage" garb adapted for current fashion. It is a confusing set of contradictory images for those growing up in this cultural milieu.

Variations on this ambivalence are also played out in our classrooms. As teachers, we expect equal effort academically from both sexes, but we may still catch ourselves accepting perceptions that are based on stereotyping. For instance, girls have been said to do better in reading, languages and humanities, while boys tend to be expected to excel in mathematics and the sciences. As a result we may be surprised when a girl states she doesn't like reading, but are merely bemused when the difficulty is in mathematics. "Oh well, that's typical," we might think. In fact, it is not typical at all. Recent reports actually indicate that young women are entering the math and science fields at the university level and beyond in far greater numbers than young men.

Now, into the midst of this somewhat mixed effort to create an egalitarian society, come students from other cultures. For many of them, there is little doubt about their roles, both as students and as members of one gender or the other. In some cultures, females of virtually any age are considered both socially and academically inferior to their male counterparts. Girls must defer to boys in the classroom, must never be too assertive and must modify their tone and form of expression to ensure that it does not reflect negatively on male members of the class.

It's easy to make snap judgments that girls who have been trained to think and act this way are meek and possibly not very bright. They seldom, if ever, volunteer an opinion, are watchful of the impression they are making, and defer to male students in discussions and group work. In addition, they rarely complain, always speak softly and agree with whatever the majority or the teacher decides. Finally, they often keep their eyes modestly lowered under all circumstances, even if fellow students and teachers alike misinterpret this.

Relationships with someone older are equally well regulated and internalized. In the dominant English-speaking cultures what used to be firm lines of decorum, such as automatically respecting elders, have blurred somewhat. In many other cultures, however, elders are considered the keepers of the wisdom and lore of the group, and are often both the guardians and teachers of the young.

This aspect of culture was driven home very directly by an incident that occurred when Sylvia was teaching in an isolated community. Things appeared to have gone seriously awry when not one parent showed up for an evening of student-led "show-and-tell" about what had been accomplished during the term.

Aside from feeling alternately mortified (at what she considered a personal failure) and outraged (because the parents just didn't seem to care), Sylvia was genuinely puzzled. The students seemed to like school and were reliable enough about getting messages home. Furthermore, they had expressed some enthusiasm about the projects they wished to display and explain.

Sylvia had overlooked the situations of the students and the historical context of schooling in the community. In the past, schooling had been seen as an impediment, something that took children away from the "real" learning that happened in the home and the community. As a result, school had a negative connotation for the parents and extended family, none of whom had ever participated more than halfheartedly in its affairs.

Furthermore, a significant number of the students in this particular class did not live with their parents. At an early age, children in this community could choose to be responsible in all matters to a member of their extended family. In many cases, this meant taking up residence with this person until they were grown and had chosen their own paths.

The individuals selected were often the grandparents or other elders of the community—and they were not at anyone's beck and call, unless they chose to be. To really clinch the embarrassing no-show, many elders did not drive or even have access to a vehicle. Nor did they have a telephone in order to call and say they couldn't—or wouldn't—come. Finally, given that the notice had not been addressed to them in the first place, could it be assumed that they had received it at all?

Needless to say, this experience taught a valuable, though somewhat painful, lesson. The next reporting period found Sylvia sitting at the feet of many of the caregivers, in their own homes, loaded down with the students' creations. While time-consuming for her, this approach provided many more opportunities for genuine communication.

When exploring the relationship between young people and their elders, it is also important to examine the relationship between students and their teachers, another form of elder. In most North American school systems, for example, serious efforts have been made to draw more men into teaching the early grades, where the vast majority of teachers have historically been women. At the same time, there have been efforts to entice more women to teach at the high school level, especially in math and science, fields that have traditionally been dominated by men.

One of the purposes of these efforts is to provide a variety of role models for students, and to eliminate the stereotype that women are better nurturers, while men deal more easily with facts and figures. Depending on how male and female roles are valued in their own cultures, however, students from other countries may or may not accept this view.

Their reactions to female and male teachers may vary considerably, according to the value their culture places on men and women. In addition, many consider it preferable to learn from someone of the same sex.

The level of respect accorded to those who are older also plays a role in determining attitudes toward teachers. Here again, it is important to examine what we take for granted. In most English-speaking countries, a degree of informality in the teacher-student relationship is fostered. This does not imply that the teacher has no authority, but rather points to the more informal and agreeable way we like to couch the reality of who's actually in charge.

Blurring the lines of status and power, both in schools and in the world at large, subtly demonstrates the firmly held belief in the equality of all, no matter what profession or life work they may have chosen. We are often bemused and even made uncomfortable by students from other cultural groups who are overly meek by English-speaking standards, jump to attention at a teacher's approach in the hallway or classroom, or remain extremely respectful and formal in all interactions.

While we may initially feel rather pleased to be teaching in a classroom in which we could hear a pin drop, the attraction of this absence of noise—including activity, laughter and talk—begins to pall in time. Many of us believe that classrooms should be busy, lively and relatively happy places, though it's worth remembering that the definition of a "happy" environment is also culturally based.

This view is not universal, however, and EAL students who arrive expecting to be taught by rote and disciplined severely for minor infractions will find a relatively casual approach difficult to understand. Some of them may think there are no rules at all. They may need to be taught, for example, that there is a big difference between going and sharpening a pencil when appropriate and climbing on bookshelves or browsing through the teacher's desk.

Even in English-speaking societies, there are individuals who believe that everything must be strictly rule-governed, even to the point of thinking that teachers should *make* them learn. Teachers need to find ways to deal with these differences in perceptions and beliefs.

The way adults relate to other adults in a given culture is also relevant. In English-speaking countries, parents and other significant adults in the students' lives are encouraged to become partners in the educational enterprise. As highlighted previously, however, we can't count on the willing and active participation of parents or guardians in school activities when dealing with parents from a variety of cultural groups.

Furthermore, when parents do come into contact with teachers and school administrators, cultural differences in nonverbal displays of dominance or submission may become evident. Some familiar scenarios come to mind.

— A parent nods and gives coverbal feedback as we provide a survey of the student's activities and progress, but never makes eye contact and doesn't appear to follow up with the at-home support to which we thought she or he had willingly agreed.
— The parent wants to hear only whether the student is well behaved and respectful of the teacher, and promises to severely punish even the most minor infractions.
— Parents gaze fondly at their offspring while the teacher tries to impress upon them how little motivation the child appears to have.
— A parent wants more homework in math even though the child is already performing well above grade-level.

Unless we're tuned in to the cultural significance of these responses, we may make the mistake of assuming these parents don't care, are too strict with and demanding of their children, or seem to agree to help with follow-up but never do. What has actually happened is that the parents have acted and interacted in culturally appropriate ways, based on their own perceptions of the way these interactions should be conducted. Appearing to agree but not following through, seeming to push too hard, and following culturally defined protocols for eye contact and coverbal feedback reflect the cultural values placed on both education and teachers.

Disclosure—Privacy

If you want to keep your friends, don't discuss religion, politics or sex! This adage highlights values and beliefs that fit on the disclosure-privacy continuum. In every cultural group, some topics are considered too private for discussion even among intimates, let alone friends and acquaintances. While these barriers are becoming highly variable within English-speaking societies, most teachers would, for example, still react negatively to being asked by the parent of a student—or the students themselves—how much money they make or what training and qualifications they have. If coverbal behavior (tone) that we're not used to is added to the mix, the potential for mistakenly assuming that the parent or student is challenging the teacher's authority or questioning her teaching ability is clearly enormous.

This happened when one of us was acting as a volunteer tutor for a local assistance organization. The patriarch of an extended family group "examined" our motivation and educational background. Absolutely no offense was intended; he was simply carrying out his duties as patriarch of the family whose members he sought to protect from real or imagined potential harm.

That these cultural ways were not ours had not occurred to him. What gave us even more insight into this particular cultural difference was his response to the fact that no form of payment was involved for the tutoring. He simply could not fathom that an individual with the excellent qualifications outlined to him would choose to work for free—for strangers—for any reason.

Teachers should be aware that students or their parents—or both—may ask about very personal matters in the same tone and with the same apparent nonchalance that might be used to inquire about the weather or how much new snow is on the ski hill. Perhaps the best approach is to consider possible deflecting statements in advance because, when on the spot, it is often difficult to remain calm and civil. In addition, consider teaching students about the sorts of questions that are and are not appropriate in the cultural milieu in which they now find themselves. Teaching them, in essence, to be bi-cultural as well as bilingual is quite worthwhile, helpful and appropriate.

Another level of the disclosure-privacy continuum relates to the solidarity of the family in relation to individual concerns. Questions about how much money you make are personal, but can be dealt with fairly simply. On the other hand, questions about, for example, the reasons for your divorce or your single marital status are another matter entirely.

In English-speaking societies, rules of decorum—who can ask what and when—govern the appropriateness of questions on matters such as this. For some, these matters remain private, whatever the cost, as they refuse opportunities to share the pain and stress with a sympathetic friend. They are matters for family only, even if this means bearing the pain in solitude because it is the family that is in crisis. Others gladly seize chances to share their sorrow in a setting of trust.

The same holds true for members of other cultures. Some, given a little encouragement, are willing to share their trials and tribulations, while others consider it almost a personal affront or a serious form of prying when they are offered a sympathetic ear.

Sometimes, as we watch students struggle to make cultural adjustments and learn a new language, we offer our assistance, only to be rebuffed or even ignored. At other times, a student may be immensely relieved to find that someone actually cares and is willing to assist, if only by filling the role of the sympathetic listener.

As teachers, we must be sensitive to these inner conflicts and make ourselves available when the burden becomes too heavy, or ensure that students know to whom they can go for help when they are ready to do so. If it is clear that a problem has been successfully resolved, some form of acknowledgment of the struggle that was involved may also be appropriate.

Direct Communication—Indirect Communication

Even when a student does approach us or accept an offer of assistance, we may still find that the interaction leaves us with new levels of miscommunication to puzzle over. Instead of laying the facts and issues before us, she may circumvent the real "problem" or couch it in terms that make it difficult for us to figure out exactly what the main issue is.

Or worse, in our hurry-up-and-get-on-with-it society, the student may go into a long and rambling explanation of the history of her arrival in her new country, the difficulty of getting settled and so on, leaving us frustrated and inclined to cut short the conversation because it seems to be going nowhere. This scenario highlights differences in communication styles, the focus of the direct-indirect continuum.

North American English-speaking societies tend to favor the direct approach. If we have a question or favor to ask, especially of someone whose status is perceived as higher than ours, we take minimal time for courteous formalities and get straight to the point.

In fact, native English-speakers have often been stereotyped by other cultures as "hello, how-are-you, good-bye-and-have-a-nice-day" types who neither care about how the person is truly feeling nor are willing to devote much valuable time to finding out. As for "having a nice day," this is considered nothing but a formula, similar to our excessive use of "please" and "thank you." It doesn't really mean anything, and certainly indicates no commitment; it is merely social lubricant to ease our many daily interactions with others.

For people from many other cultures, however, this kind of direct, to-the-point approach is considered inappropriate and rude. Their approaches to communication, even when the problem is urgent, may appear to be extremely formal, very indirect and even vague.

Three Cups of Tea, a book based on the story of Greg Mortenson's work to build schools in Pakistan and beyond, illustrates this difference. While we are aware there are differences in how people conduct business—even within the North American context—the exemplar of sitting to drink tea and discussing, for an extended period of time, anything and everything except the purpose of the meeting would likely make many of us grit our teeth with impatience. The explanation is embedded in what is valued most, the end product or the relationships.

It is the relationships that are so charmingly highlighted in the explanation of the book's title. In summary, the value-embedded process is as follows. When with the Balti, the first cup of tea you share makes you nothing more than a stranger who is given the hospitality due to all strangers, the second cup makes you an honored guest, while the third cup makes you part of the family.

All of us have probably heard stories of the difficulties experienced by English-speaking business people who have traveled abroad to create economic and entrepreneurial alliances. "Our" team immediately wants to start negotiating and discussing equitable ways of creating partnerships, while "their"

102

team appears to be stonewalling, more concerned with maintaining harmony among its representatives than with clinching the deal.

Even the language we use to describe interactions such as this point to the direct and forceful nature of what are considered "Western" approaches. No rudeness or disrespect is intended. Rather, people have been trained not to waste the time of a busy executive or other high-ranking official with what may seem to be frivolities.

To further complicate matters, consider all this in the light of two more typical interactions. Imagine a job interview in which the candidate may be perceived to be avoiding answering the questions, and instead talks about his early life and other interests. What is at play here?

Next, consider parent-teacher conferences. We are product oriented for the most part—as in the job interview—yet switch to a process orientation with regard to discussing a child's progress. Parents, who only seem to want to know what the child's marks are and how they rank in the class, may be judged rather harshly. One might cite an old adage on behalf of immigrant learners—"sometimes you just can't win."

In addition, when conflicts do arise, the North American approach to dealing with them tends to be frank and open. We "lay our cards on the table," as it were, viewing alternative responses as needlessly circumspect. If someone has been trained to assume that anyone who doesn't immediately "play it straight" must be hiding something, the seeds of suspicion may be sown.

Related to this issue are the strategies used to try to persuade someone—in a more informal setting than the boardroom—to adopt our point of view. The fact that most of us think it is appropriate to try to talk someone into a particular approach or way of doing things speaks volumes. Given that persuasion is acceptable, it is considered quite appropriate to wheedle and cajole to get our own way. Many cultural groups view tactics such as these with a great deal of suspicion.

In the classroom, teachers often manage the environment by using persuasive tactics, whether this is to encourage students to try something or to intervene in a conflict in an attempt to create order and a measure of conviviality. We should be aware that some students might see approaches such as this as inappropriate, or even totally incomprehensible.

In English-speaking cultures, face-to-face interaction is the preferred way of dealing with others. In many other cultures, however, a form of go-between is used, and the higher the status of the negotiators, the less likely they are to consent to meet face to face. Though face-to-face interaction is the norm in parent-teacher conferences, we need to be conscious that this direct approach may create discomfort. This consciousness can go a long way toward avoiding serious misunderstandings.

A final note on the direct-indirect communication continuum relates to competition and cooperation. Though this issue has been dealt with in relation to schooling, it is raised here in relation to the overall approach to interaction of any sort. If your personal approach is basically conciliatory and cooperative, you are unlikely to be seriously concerned about where your child ranks in the class. Rather, you are more interested in hearing about whether he is cooperative, helpful and gets along with his peers. If, however, you thrive on competition, high marks and excellence in all areas may be very important to you, and expected of your offspring as well.

Though these issues are not necessarily culture-based and may well be individual and personal, there is an understandable tendency for some immigrant parents to be very concerned about the academic success of their children. Often the parents view schooling as a golden opportunity to improve their socio-economic standing by sheer will and hard work, and they are very intolerant of children who do not appear to strive as hard as they do themselves. As we saw in Chapter Five, this is particularly troublesome for us when we understand that the child in question will simply never be able to come up to the ambitious expectations of the parents.

Because the bias in North American English-speaking cultures is to encourage children to work hard at school while making sure they have time to play and have fun, a parent who demands that homework be sent home from Kindergarten may come into conflict with the teacher. The teacher's efforts to understand the parents' backgrounds and circumstances, combined with the parents' efforts to find out about the philosophy of our education systems, will go a long way toward lessening the misunderstandings that may occur and better support the needs of the child caught in the middle.

Flexible Time—Time As a Commodity

Differing perceptions of time were mentioned briefly in Chapter Four. At this point, a more detailed analysis of culture-specific attitudes toward time is in order. Again, this represents a continuum of approaches, with time counted virtually by the second at one end, and time as a very flexible entity over which imposed control is seen as neither necessary nor appropriate at the other.

Time is very important in most English-speaking societies, and tends to be "used up" or budgeted according to fairly rigid conventions. For example, suppose you are late for a luncheon appointment. Lateness of a minute or two requires a polite apology, lateness of several minutes' calls for profuse apologies and probably an explanation. If you will be significantly more than 10 minutes late, you are expected to make an effort to call ahead. If it is a business lunch, this protocol is even more important. If it is a job interview, lateness of no more than a few seconds is tolerable—if you wish to be considered for the position.

By contrast, in some cultures the correct time for something important is flexible and elusive, perhaps gauged by unwritten religious or spiritual traditions, by the tides, by the time of year or by the position of the sun. For example, the time to eat may be governed by when a person is hungry, not by a clock on the wall or a wristwatch; the time to plant or harvest may be determined in an equally non-specific way. In relation to doing business—consider the three cups of tea example in the previous continuum—the time to get down to business is often incomprehensible.

People raised in North American English-speaking cultures, socialized in a hurry-up world view, have run into conflict with societies that do not see time as a commodity that is constantly in danger of being used up. With all the good intentions in the world, for example, this approach has led to some notable agricultural disasters in which experts from other continents have offered assistance in food production to less industrialized nations. Their failure to trust the folklore of the people to whom the help was offered overrode what turned out to be very accurate predictions of the right time to plant or let fields lie fallow.

There is a children's story about a young bull named Ferdinand, who is preoccupied with enjoying nature. Rather than getting on with learning—in his case butting heads with the other young bulls in the field in preparation for entering the bull ring—he prefers to sit under a tree and smell the flowers. Though the theme of this story deals with pacifism and aggression, it also speaks to differences in the concept of time; time to simply *be* as opposed to time to *do*.

Parents, particularly in some social circles, literally fill their children's days with things to do—music lessons, craft classes, sports—until there is little room left for the children to simply *be*. In fact, simply "hanging out" is often considered somewhat suspect, an absence of profitable activity that will all too likely lead to no good. Ironically, a common complaint today is that children do not seem to know how to entertain themselves. Perhaps this is because every waking moment is planned for them or filled with entertainment.

In some cultures, however, the personal interactions— whether these are talking, singing or just sitting—that occur in time that is simply to *be* are considered much more valuable than achieving X by timeframe Y. When children from these backgrounds come to our classes, misunderstandings are bound to occur. These students might seem to ignore deadlines for handing in assignments or think getting to school on time is not vital. In addition, their parents could, by our standards, be seriously late for meetings with school officials.

Time is also extremely important when it comes to face-to-face interactions. For example, North Americans tend to measure the wait-time between speakers in minute particles. While everyone has talked—or, should we say, listened—to someone who never allows the speaker to complete a thought, strict conventions usually govern how we take turns in conversation. What may not be as clear is how the length of the wait-time may vary from culture to culture.

As we saw in Chapter Four, people from a culture in which it's customary to take the time to think carefully through what one wants to say require a significantly longer wait-time compared with those people from cultures where everybody seems to talk at once.

In addition, if it is appropriate in a particular culture to have long silences to ponder, gaze or simply be, the protocols of turn taking become even more complex and are often disrupted when those who aren't used to this etiquette leap into the conversation prematurely. The comfort level of silence in the presence of others was also discussed in Chapter Four but deserves a brief reminder here, as it is a key element of our day-to-day interactions with students in the classroom.

Imagine yourself guiding a class discussion. The usual few are ready to talk instantly, but many seldom take part actively. It would be easy to conclude that some of those who don't contribute do not understand, while others have not done the reading or homework and are, therefore, unable to participate. It's worth remembering, however, that expressing opinions in class may be completely alien to some of the reluctant participants, who may need time to think about a response because they have never been asked to give an opinion.

For students who are used to classrooms in which participation means listening and taking notes, responses to requests to say what they think will not come easily. Even when students have been asked to express an opinion, they may be accustomed to giving a careful response that is the result of much thought.

A final aspect of differing views of time relates to orientation or direction. English-speaking cultures tend to be very future-oriented. We look forward to the future, plan our activities on this basis and strive to accomplish X, Y and Z by some fixed point in the future (when I graduate, when I get a promotion, when I retire).

Though we don't ignore the lessons of the past, they tend not to be the primary force that motivates us to act in a particular way. This fits well with the learning-by-doing and trial-and-error classroom philosophies that were previously mentioned.

For people from many cultures, however, this lack of reverence for and adherence to what was done in the past and learned from those experiences is difficult to comprehend. This orientation to the past and what it has to teach us every waking moment needs to be acknowledged and considered when dealing with parents of EAL students. Although they may fully understand that they are now in a new culture and country where there are some different rules of conduct and approaches to teaching and learning, their own orientation may continue to be quite different. This is yet another instance of where our goal as educators is not to supplant the home languages and cultures of our learners, but to help them live and learn in two languages and cultures.

The Core of Our Humanity

In summary, our values and belief systems are at the core of what makes us human. Everything we say and do is motivated at some conscious or unconscious level by what we believe is right and appropriate at a given moment. Should others with whom we interact not value what *we* value and believe in equally, it will color both our interactions with them and our feelings about them as individuals.

Unfortunately, these perceptions tend to be judgmental, remain tenaciously constant, deepen with experience, and become highly selective. We tend to see what we have been taught from birth to see. This chapter has attempted to highlight some of the key areas where differences in perception can lead to miscommunication. We strongly believe that recognizing our own cultural values, and increasing our understanding and awareness that others may perceive these same values quite differently, will help us in our work with EAL learners from around the globe.

Ronald Inglehart has encapsulated a number of the qualities children can be encouraged to learn. It may be a useful exercise, before you find yourself speaking with parents and colleagues about the qualities you are hoping to engender in your students, to examine your own biases in this regard. Review the list that follows and prioritize the qualities. It is very likely that your colleagues, trained to teach in the same school system, might have these in a different order. How much more then might the parents of immigrant children view these in a different order of priority? The following list of qualities comes from Inglehart's extensive *World Values Survey* books and website and, in an abridged form, includes:

— determination
— feeling of responsibility
— hard work
— imagination
— independence
— obedience
— respect
— thrift
— tolerance
— unselfishness

The seven chapters we have read so far have considered a variety of specific social, economic and cultural issues that make up the context in which we welcome new EAL learners into our classrooms and schools. This doesn't, however, cover all the questions that classroom teachers can and do ask. While much is beyond the scope and purpose of this book, addressing some of these classroom concerns is the topic of the final chapter.

Review and Extend

— Mentally review a recent misunderstanding at work, on your way to work, in the classroom or at home. Consider the event through new eyes. Was there a conflict based on different assumptions that were never openly expressed?
— What cultural stereotypes are you aware of, and where have they come from? Did anyone ever try to justify them to you? How would you respond now?
— What are some differences that cause friction at work among colleagues, or in your classroom among students? Could this friction be due to differences in values and belief systems?

— What are your expectations for your students in terms of the five continua outlined in this chapter? Are your students complying with your perceptions of where they should be located on these continua? Consider, in particular, those students with whom you find it a challenge to deal.

— Read at least three different versions of the Cinderella story. Review the differences among them in terms of the perceptions of gender roles and perceptions of beauty. How do these relate to current perceptions held by your students? This could develop into a fascinating teachable moment.

— How do your learners know who is in charge in the classroom? How would newcomers to your classroom know who is in charge and what the rules are? Are they posted? Whose rules are they? What happens if someone infringes on these rules?

— It is said that patience is a virtue. How consistently do you exhibit this trait? When are you infinitely patient and when are you less so? Does it depend on the task at hand, what the issue requiring patience is, or whatever other factors impinge on your ability to be patient with learners? How do your learners know what to expect from you? Or could they possibly have grounds for considering you unpredictable?

— Consider the issue of time in terms of student response time. Recall a language you learned through several school years. Now formulate a simple question such as asking what my name is in that language. Notice the time it takes you to review mentally how to formulate that response. Perhaps you have to recall the appropriate vocabulary, what tense the verb should be, how to formulate it into a question and whether you are ad-dressing an equal or a child. Unless you are using that language daily, it is likely that you had to consider several factors with care and spend at least a few seconds formulating your response. Given that in fact you were actually required to complete the task in this book's dominant language you did not also have to first figure out what was being asked. This small example is only a fragment of what EAL learners have to do all day long. Is it any wonder that their response times can seem slow to us?

— If you have not already done so, rank order the attributes listed at the end of the chapter. According to the *World Values Survey* these are what parents strongly encourage in their children. However, in what priority order they are placed varies across both groups and individuals. For example, where would you place obedience as opposed to independence in terms of your own children? Which would you most desire for the learners in your classroom? Would your ranking parallel that of others teaching at your school? Which would you think is the highest rank for the parents of your students—would each parent have a different priority order?

. . . .

CHAPTER EIGHT

PUTTING IT ALL TOGETHER

Lord grant me the serenity to accept the things I cannot
change, the courage to change the things I can, and the
wisdom to know the difference.

Author Unknown

What are the implications of the material in this
book for the busy classroom teacher? If all these elements of
communication are really important, and more and more
students are not members of the dominant English-speaking
culture, does this mean that we are constantly dealing with miscommunication?

Surely, we teachers cannot be expected to learn all the nonverbal and cultural aspects of communication of every cultural
group represented in our classrooms? Shouldn't students from
other countries be expected to learn to function and live in their
new culture? Shouldn't the onus be on them to learn new communication and behavior patterns? Furthermore, how do we
teach nonverbal and cross-cultural communication? Which
culture and behavior patterns do we use as a model? Finally,
even if we attempted this, how could we avoid implying that
other patterns of behavior are, therefore, somehow less acceptable?

These are just some of the questions that may have crossed
your mind as you read the previous chapters. In this final
chapter, some of the key issues that confront teachers who find
themselves working with new EAL learners will be addressed. By

posing some commonly asked questions, we hope to review and highlight the most useful points to consider in your day-to-day dealings with these new members of your class.

Where do I start?

Start with yourself. The skills and experience you bring to the classroom, combined with a willingness to venture into a relatively unfamiliar area of teaching and learning, are your greatest assets. Being yourself will provide a positive model for both the new EAL learners and the rest of the class.

Be aware! In this book, we have tried to highlight some of the complexities of culture and communication. Becoming a careful and sympathetic observer of the new students in your class will enable you to become aware of subtleties of behavior that might otherwise have escaped you. Without this awareness, unfortunate misunderstandings between you and the new EAL students—and among class members—can, and will, occur.

Start with the simple things. If you were new to your school, what places, routines and regulations would you need to be aware of to function effectively? For example, the location of washrooms and the office, gymnasium and library could easily be recorded on a map of the school. (The layout of many urban high schools is so complex that even some teachers feel they need a map to find their way around!) In addition, routines we take for granted, such as assigning a locker, supplying or buying a lock for it, and using it to store equipment needed for school, may be completely unfamiliar and baffling to new students.

In elementary schools, an additional issue must be considered. Many elementary classrooms have a cloakroom that includes small, open cubbyholes for personal possessions such as extra books, lunch kits and the like. North American children learn very early that these cubbies are the property of the students assigned to them. As a result, they have been trained from early on that one does not take things from other students' cubbies or put one's own things in them. Yet the cubbies are wide open.

Children from other cultures may not feel that their things are safe in this kind of open space. Some may feel the same way about their desks and, as a result, carry everything home every

113

day. Obviously, this practice should be discussed with the new students, who may need time to adjust to this novel approach, especially if they are refugees who are used to guarding their few possessions for fear of losing them. On the other hand, new students may be under the impression that everything in all the cubbyholes is common property. This can lead to equally challenging behaviors for you to sort through.

Recess and lunchtimes may also be new events for students, especially those in elementary schools. Secondary students are more likely to watch carefully and follow the crowd when figuring out how to behave, but elementary students may need help in a couple of areas. First, young learners may need to be taught that recess is for playing out of doors and for eating a small snack, if appropriate. They may also require explanations, and even demonstrations, of expectations for behavior in the playground and on equipment. Some schools designate specific playground areas for various age groups, and rules may govern when specific groups can use the basketball hoops, swings, adventure playground equipment and so on.

In addition, both recess and lunch are open-ended timeframes that may lead immigrant children to believe initially that school is over for the day and they ought to go home. Further, the idea of eating your midday meal with anyone other than your family is another behavior that may need to be explained through modeling and perhaps even with the assistance of an interpreter.

Be helpful and patient. EAL students require a tremendous amount of assistance in many areas as they begin to learn about new cultural and social roles and expectations. It is important to recognize, however, that the new learners may initially be so overwhelmed that they are unlikely to ask many questions, even when the answers would be very helpful. Consider how exhausting it must be to be totally immersed in a foreign language, expected to figure out the conventions of the new environment into which you have been unceremoniously thrust, and asked to function normally as a student. The wisest approach may be simply to ensure that you are available when these students are able to process more new information.

Perhaps the best possible advice we can give is to suggest you follow the KISS (keep it simple, silly) principle. The sheer volume of input to which these new students are subjected in the first few weeks of school precludes them from absorbing elaborate and detailed explanations. When they are ready to process more information, they will let you know—and you will have avoided repeating yourself and feeling frustrated because they "still don't seem to understand."

What else can I do to help EAL learners adjust to my classroom?

Acknowledge that the adjustments are many, real and that they vary from student to student. EAL learners are attempting to cope simultaneously with the loss of everything known and familiar to them and the fear and anxiety that any form of change can inspire. For example, your acceptance of the fact that, at first, these learners may be silent and appear relatively unresponsive in the classroom will go a long way toward easing the transitions they are trying to make.

There is a delicate balance, however, between displaying empathy and understanding during an adjustment period and spoon-feeding. As the teacher, you have a responsibility to help new students understand and deal with the expectations of their new school.

Make your expectations clear. Do not assume anything. Policies relating to, for example, school attendance, including punctuality, and expectations about completing assignments may not necessarily be familiar to newcomers. In addition, remember that the EAL learners in our midst are still struggling simply to understand in a new language. Reinforcing oral instructions in writing or in graphic form is often a great help.

Personal planners are becoming a common tool in many schools and are used even by young learners. Planners teach the basics of time management and reinforce good work habits, careful planning and self-reliance. A tool like this can help already overloaded EAL learners in two ways: it helps teach them good work habits, and it is a visual reminder of what was said and done in class. Even if the teacher must record the data on the pages at first, students will quickly come to understand the purpose of a planner and begin to complete it on their own.

As a result of discussions with classroom teachers, especially at the upper intermediate and secondary levels, we drafted the

115

following letter to help newly integrated EAL students understand classroom expectations. You may find it helpful to
compose a similar letter for the new EAL learners in your
classroom. Needless to say, this is of value only when the
students have mastered basic communication skills in English,
unless you have access to cultural and linguistic interpreters. In
that case, whether in print, orally or both, such information
would be helpful for your new learners.

Dear (Integrated EAL Student):

I want to help you do your best in my class. Here are some
things to do and think about so that you can do your best.

1. Write clearly so that I can understand.
2. I know that the way you pronounce words in English
   won't be perfect, but I want to understand, so please
   help me by SPEAKING slowly and clearly.
3. I will try not to speak too quickly. LISTEN carefully.
   Make sure you know *what* homework is assigned,
   when it is to be handed in, and *when* the next test or
   review is going to be.
4. To make sure you have UNDERSTOOD the lesson, talk
   about it with someone else in the class.
5. Do all the READING NECESSARY for this subject. Some
   material is hard to understand. Therefore, you may
   have to read it *many times* or *ask* a teacher for help. The
   more you read, the faster your English will improve
   and the easier reading will become.
6. ORGANIZE your notes. Have one book or section for
   each subject. Keep all handouts from your teachers in
   the order they are given to you. Writing a date on each
   as you receive it will help you do this.
7. HAND in all assignments on the day they are due. Talk
   to the teacher if you are not finished.
8. Keep a VOCABULARY list of important terms for each
   subject and learn the meanings as soon as possible.
   Remember that many English words have more than
   one meaning.

9. ASK QUESTIONS WHEN YOU DON'T UNDERSTAND. You can do this either in class or after class. I know this is hard, but it is important.

Your teacher

The importance of establishing clear, consistent routines and expectations, as well as the students' continuing need for feedback and support, cannot be overemphasized. In fact, this kind of clarity and consistency is valuable for everyone in the classroom.

Take time to talk to the entire class about how difficult change and adjustment can be. Teachable moments, such as when someone announces the arrival of a new brother or sister or that a friend has moved away, can become worthwhile springboards to discussion of the event, as well as the ambivalent feelings that may surround it. An in-depth exploration of issues such as these can also be tied to curriculum areas such as literature, guidance and the social sciences.

At the same time, make some of the cultural and communication issues explicit for the entire class. Throughout this book, we have talked about the importance of developing an awareness of the complexities of culture and communication. Not only can English-speaking students benefit from insights into their own patterns of behavior and social interaction, but the EAL learners will also benefit. Their own way of being will be validated, and they will gain an awareness of culturally appropriate ways to interact in the English-speaking context. As we have mentioned, your role as a teacher includes helping the EAL learners to be *both* bilingual and bi-cultural.

What can I do to include the EAL learners in classroom academic learning activities?

Research in the field of second language acquisition tells us that it takes from two to nine years to achieve academic norms in the second language that are consistent with the students' age and academic level. Given this extended time frame, providing support for the EAL learners in your classroom is clearly a long-term commitment. Here are a few suggestions for providing the kind of continuing assistance they need if they are to reach their academic potential in this new language:

— Clearly state—and write out—your expectations. For assignments and projects, ensure that EAL learners have seen a model of what is expected and have been given clear, step-by-step instructions—both oral and written.
— Use learning partners, buddies and teacher-selected groups.
— Allow extra time (and rehearsals) for EAL students to formulate oral answers, but don't let them off the hook; make it clear that you expect that they will speak, given the time to develop a response. Their receptive skills (the ability to understand most of what's going on) will develop much more quickly than their productive skills (the ability to talk about what has been learned or understood).
— Allow extra time for assignments, and encourage draft submissions to you or a buddy or peer tutor. At first, you may also wish to consider varying the length and complexity of assignments, as well as the kind of responses expected.
— Be encouraging, both verbally and nonverbally. (See the examples offered in Chapter Two).
— If the objective of a lesson is to ensure that students understand content, evaluate their speaking and writing for ideas, not grammar. For example, a poorly constructed paragraph that nonetheless demonstrates comprehension of the concept deserves a passing grade. On the other hand, if you focus on grammar, the same paragraph would be viewed in quite a different light.
— It's worth noting that teaching grammar for grammar's sake has repeatedly proven to be a poor vehicle for promoting efficient language learning. An emphasis on content-based language learning, on the other hand, has been shown to be highly successful. This holds true even for those new to the English language.
— Give praise and marks for effort, enthusiasm, attitude and participation, not only for "perfection." Remember,

however, that members of some cultural groups can find any form of praise very discomfiting. Noting a student's reaction to praise can provide an important guide for future interactions.

— When possible, say a student's name before asking the question and keep others on task by encouraging them to be responsible for helping the EAL learner comprehend.

— Use graphic organizers, (such as tables, charts, and diagrams), as well as visual and concrete materials in your presentations, and encourage students to use them in their own work.

— Get to know the students and use them as resources. They come to your classroom with considerable background knowledge that can help them access new learning, provided you are prepared to help them build the connections to their background knowledge using their new language.

— Provide ample preparation material, such as reading lists, at the outset of a new topic or unit of study. Encouraging EAL learners to pre-read new material will facilitate their comprehension and encourage them to participate more in class.

— Distinguish between assessment *for* learning (to see what needs to be taught) and assessment *of* learning (to see what has been learned).

— Use learning journals to help students synthesize what has been learned and to assist you in finding out what needs more emphasis, such as teaching, re-teaching and reviewing.

When considering these suggestions, it's important to keep in mind the effect of culture on the way students and teachers interact. The *Teacher Behavior and Expectations* chart on the next page provides a useful overview of cultural issues that may impact on these interactions.

For the purposes of illustration, the chart pairs common practices in North American classrooms with a somewhat artificial opposite extreme. As explained in Chapter Seven, the point

on the continuum where each of us feels comfortable is a matter
of personal style overlaid with cultural norms.

Teacher Behavior and Expectations	
North American	Other Possibilities
Praise is overt.	Praise is embarrassing.
Eye contact is expected.	Eye contact is rude.
Physical contact is normal, especially with younger children.	Physical contact is taboo, especially between sexes.
Physical distance (personal space bubble) is 40-70 cm (1.5-2.5 ft.).	Physical distance is either much closer or much farther apart.
Silence is never prolonged; an instant answer is expected.	Silence is comfortable and can imply thought.
Most feelings may be displayed, but not necessarily acted upon.	Feelings must be hidden or, in other cases, displayed with gusto.
Intimate topics can be discussed openly (few are very private).	Taboo topics are highly variable and culturally defined.
Punctuality is prized.	Time is flexible.
Relative status is not emphasized.	Status is very important.
Roles are loosely defined.	Role expectations are strict.
Competition is desirable.	Group harmony is desired.
Politeness is routine but lapses occur and are forgiven. "Thank you" is sufficient.	Politeness and proper conduct are paramount, especially in children. Gifts of thanks are offered and expected.

North American	Other Possibilities
Education is for everyone.	Education is first and foremost for males.

The EAL students in my class rarely become involved in extra-curricular activities. Because these activities are a significant part of school life in North America, how can I encourage and promote their participation?

Participation—or the lack of it—is often a result of differing cultural values, economic constraints, or a combination of the two. When you are dealing with students from a culture that does not believe in the educational value of play, including sports, you cannot expect them to participate immediately or enthusiastically.

In addition, many EAL students must help with family responsibilities, from child minding to working at a part-time job. Given that they also need to complete school assignments, this may leave little time for extracurricular activities.

Nevertheless, much anecdotal evidence suggests that encouraging EAL learners to participate in extracurricular activities supports their social, emotional, cultural and linguistic adjustment. The benefits cited by teachers include gaining opportunities to use English to speak and interact outside the classroom, learning North American norms for team play, and getting physical exercise. Some teachers have also noted that joining the school choir results in a dramatic improvement in pronunciation.

Here are some suggestions for promoting EAL student participation in extracurricular activities:

— Allow EAL students time to adjust to the whole idea of extracurricular involvement. During the entire first semester or even year at a new school, EAL learners may be far too busy simply acclimatizing and trying to keep up to consider adding more to their schedules. Once this initial adjustment period is over, they are more likely to be receptive to the idea of becoming involved in other activities.

— Capitalize on EAL student strengths. Find out about their interests and abilities and encourage them in these directions. For example, many students arrive with well-developed skills in specific sports. A personal introduction to a coach or sponsoring teacher can help foster enthusiasm and participation. Other students may be skilled in areas such as board games. If, for instance, there is a chess club in the school, this may be attractive to some learners. One teacher found it helpful to actually go with the EAL learners to the organizational meeting, as she had been told that while some students were interested, they were unsure where to go and what would happen when they arrived.

— Buddy up where feasible. Participating in extracurricular activities involves taking a certain amount of risk. Pairing EAL students with a classmate who is also interested in a particular activity can help them overcome their anxiety about taking this risk.

— Sponsor or promote new activities. The interests of EAL learners may provide a catalyst for creating new activities or clubs in the school. If the EAL learners are the experts, it will not only raise their self-esteem but also promote interaction with students throughout the school.

— Help the parents of EAL students understand the value of extracurricular activities. Though the students themselves are a useful starting point, remember that their parents need to understand the value of these kinds of activities in order to sanction them and encourage their children to participate. Despite your efforts, it's always possible that parents will approve only certain activities and deny their children permission to participate in others for social, economic or cultural reasons.

— Help parents understand that co-curricular activities are also an important aspect of school life. These may include swimming programs, field studies, special camping experiences and some elements of physical education programs such as golf or water sports. Members of some cultures feel that only text-oriented classroom activities are educationally valid. Take time to explain the relationship between these non-academic activities and the curriculum to EAL parents.

How do I help the parents of EAL learners to become involved in school life?

Parents may be reluctant to participate in their children's education for a number of reasons. These could include:

— Fear because of their own lack of proficiency in English.
— The need for both parents to work, sometimes at more than one job.
— The presence of younger family members at home (many mothers would never consider leaving their children with a stranger, nor would they consider it appropriate to bring the younger child along).
— The feeling that they have nothing to contribute.
— The valuing of parental engagement in education is an unfamiliar concept.

Though some parents may seem reluctant to become involved, this should not be seen as a lack of interest in, and valuing of, education *per se*. Most immigrant parents consider education extremely important. In fact, improving their children's access to an excellent education is often an important factor in a family's decision to emigrate. Despite the difficulties we may encounter, we need to encourage parents to become partners in their children's education at whatever levels they can manage. Here are some suggested strategies for doing this:

— Begin a consistent flow of communication. School-wide or classroom-based newsletters, translated into the students' home languages if possible, help develop parents' awareness of what is happening at school. In addition, regularly sending notes to parents that praise their children's accomplishments, both academic and in other areas, helps establish a positive relationship between teacher and parent.
— Inviting comments and information about how parents would like to be involved can help establish and maintain communication. Providing parents with a checklist

of possible options is often a good idea. Encouraging them to participate in various events such as field studies or special celebrations also helps improve their understanding of the new educational milieu.

— Parents are often very willing to help with homework, but aren't at all sure how to go about it. To help them help their children with assignments, provide useful and clear information, and design assignments that will encourage family discussion and participation.

— Home reading programs have proven very successful for all learners. Research makes it clear that the act of reading aloud with a significant older person enhances reading skills. This holds true even when it is not the target language that is being used. However, it should be noted that the dominant North American norm of reading with children from an early age is not a universal one. In many cultures it is far more usual to sit together and tell stories or listen to the radio and discuss what is heard. Asking the caregivers from such cultural environments to become readers may not be an option even if they are literate in their home languages, as they may not be comfortable with this somewhat unfamiliar activity.

— Value the home languages. Current research into the way children learn language points to the importance of maintaining and strengthening their proficiency in their home language. Encourage parents to continue to use and develop their children's first language. This may include reading bilingual books and books in the home language, as well as sharing stories, legends and songs.

How can I help the rest of the students develop an understanding of the EAL learners in the class?

Never underestimate the power of the teachable moment. Seizing every opportunity to discuss issues as they arise can benefit the entire class. For example, a news event that is being discussed in class may be interpreted differently as a result of different values and belief systems. Miscommunications, which are bound to occur and may be based on a misunderstanding or simply different approaches to a task, can provide opportunities for everyone to learn and gain insights.

Examine the curriculum for possible theme-based issues. The existing curriculum contains a range of opportunities for examining the larger issues related to immigration, change and adjustment. Studying the changes brought about by waves of immigrants over the past decades and centuries, for example, can highlight for all students that the current influx of immigrants is not unique and that it may indeed have a number of benefits.

Explicit teaching of cultural understandings can be beneficial for all learners. Rarely do we think about, let alone teach, specific aspects of our culture. On occasion, there may be a place for highlighting both similarities and differences in the way people from different cultural groups view the world. It is enlightening for both English-speaking and EAL students to think consciously about and discuss things that they have been taking for granted, or have assumed to be universals.

An example of this might be asking questions. By responding positively, we encourage children, from a very young age, to ask questions. To students raised in a culture where observation is the norm, asking questions will be a completely new concept. In essence, they will need to learn how to ask questions. Alternatively, some learners will have been strongly encouraged not to ask questions, especially of their elders. Asking them to suddenly question and discuss what the authority in the classroom is teaching would be seen as rude and disrespectful.

How can I possibly teach them all they need to know?

You can't. Determine what is reasonable and offer it in small chunks. This will help you develop reasonable expectations of yourself as well as enabling your students to assimilate the information as they perceive the need for it. Developing your own perspective on what you can reasonably expect to accomplish will give the EAL learners the time they need, without neglecting the needs of the rest of the class.

Ask for help. Students in your class or school, colleagues, resource people in the school and community, as well as parents, can contribute to your work with EAL learners. While the onus may be on you to set up tutoring programs or other approaches, both you and the learners will ultimately benefit greatly.

Listen to your EAL students. A survey of 180 EAL learners in an urban high school asked them to identify what teachers could do to help them as they struggled to cope with content materials in their second language. Their responses included the following:

— Write things, including homework, on the board.
— Slow down the speed when speaking at length.
— Don't isolate us at the back of the room.
— Ask me to stay for help (I'm too shy to ask).
— Encourage us to be active in class (it helps me get courage).
— Give us easier questions and passages to read out loud at first.
— Give us more than one day for homework assignments.
— Review work and write important things on the chalkboard.
— Help us to work in groups.
— Take an interest in me other than just my marks.
— Hand out notes so I can study at home.
— Encourage other students to work with us.
— Have lots of patience.
— Don't judge me by my English.
— Don't treat us like strangers.
— Check to see if I understand.
— Explain difficult vocabulary and give us a vocabulary sheet with meanings (it takes so long to look up so many words).
— Don't insult us when we don't understand.
— Please don't say I'm not listening. I really am.
— Smile.

In addition to providing some useful suggestions and confirming that the students know their own needs, these responses also serve as a poignant reminder that EAL learners have needs that go far beyond acquiring language and learning subject matter.

Practice in basic skills can benefit everyone. Though the EAL learners in your class will need far more practice and specific language-based activities than native English speakers, the opportunity for all students to hone their skills should not be overlooked. In fact, you may find that EAL students develop a superior grasp of underlying grammatical structures. Class-wide skill sessions may actually afford them a rare opportunity to assist their English-speaking peers, instead of the other way around.

A Final Word

The key message of this book may be summed up as, "Take nothing for granted." Or, as we often remind ourselves, "Assume nothing!" Cultural norms accepted in much of the English-speaking world are not necessarily a reliable measure when interpreting the actions of others, or for assuming that our own actions will be understood. Nor can they be used to predict what will happen in a given situation. As teachers, we need to transcend our own subconscious cultural training and see ways of operating and interacting with the world as one approach among many.

This book attempts to increase teacher awareness of culturally different behavior patterns and how these can affect daily life in the multicultural classroom. Increasing our understanding of these differences does not imply that we must accept them as our own. It does imply, however, that heightened sensitivity to different ways of viewing and interacting with the world will enhance our ability to build bridges between and among the cultural groups in our classrooms.

While we have tried to make it clear that it is unrealistic to expect teachers to acquire languages and cultural norms from around the world, our learners, on the other hand, are in the process of learning to operate in more than one language and in at least two cultures. Being bi- or multilingual as well as bi- or multicultural is exactly what they need in order to be able to take their places effectively in their new homeland.

In closing, we would like to leave you with one final quotation, one that encapsulates our values and beliefs and the philosophy upon which the tenets of this book are based.

I do not want my house walled in on all sides and my windows stuffed. I want the cultures of all lands to be blown about my house as freely as possible, but I refuse to be blown off my feet by any.

Mahatma Ghandi

. . . .

REFERENCES AND RESOURCES

The following resource lists are in two main parts. Noted first are all the specific references we used and to which we have referred throughout the book. Secondly, though this book's focus is not on details of method or strategies, for your convenience some useful references and practical resources have been provided within the following broad categories:

— General References
— Learning More
— Culture and Communication
— Working with Special Learners
— Strategies, Resources and Materials
— Websites for Teachers and Learners

Please note that where links from the World Wide Web are included a word of caution is in order. While all the links were working when we cited the source at the time of writing, there are constant elements of reorganization, with the result that a particular link might not work when you attempt to find it. Usually, though, the article is available at a new web address. For this reason we have included as much information as possible, including the full titles when available, to allow you to search for the information in more than one way.

General References

Banks, James A. and C.A. McGee Banks, eds. *Multicultural Education: Issues and Perspectives*. 7th. edition. Hoboken, NJ: John Wiley & Sons, 2010.

B.C Ministry of Education. *Students from Refugee Backgrounds: A Guide for Teachers and Schools*. October, 2009. <www.bced.gov.bc.ca/esl/refugees_teachers_guide.pdf>

Citizenship and Immigration Canada <www.cic.gc.ca>

Cummins, Jim. *BICS and CALP*. <www.iteachilearn.org/cummins/bicscalp.html>

Cummins, Jim. *Bilingual Children's Mother Tongue: Why Is It Important for Education?* <www.iteachilearn.org/cummins/mother.htm>

Freeman, Yvonne, S.D.E. Freeman and S.P. Mercuri. *Closing the Achievement Gap: How to Reach Limited-Formal Schooling and Long-Term English Learners*. Portsmouth, NH: Heinemann, 2002.

Gunderson, Lee. *English-Only Instruction and Immigrant Students in Secondary Schools: A Critical Examination*. Mahwah, NJ: Lawrence Erlbaum Associates, 2007.

Gunderson, Lee. *ESL(ELL) Literacy Instruction: A Guidebook to Theory and Practice*. 2nd. edition. New York, NY: Routledge, 2009.

Hall, Edward T. *The Silent Language*. New York, NY: Doubleday, 1973.

Hall, Edward T. *Beyond Culture*. New York, NY: Doubleday/ Anchor Books, 1976.

Hall, Edward T. *The Hidden Dimension*. New York, NY: Doubleday/Anchor Books, 1990.

Hamayan, Else, B. Marler, C. Sanchez-Lopez and J. Damico. *Special Education Considerations for English Language Learners: Delivering a Continuum of Services.* Philadelphia, PA: Caslon Inc., 2007.

Harris, Carole R. *Identifying and Serving Recent Immigrant Children Who Are Gifted.* ERIC DIGEST (EC E520), 1993. <eric.hoagiesgifted.org/e520.html>

Henry, Frances and C. Tator. *The Colour of Democracy: Racism in Canadian Society.* 4th edition. Toronto, ON: Cengage Learning Inc., Nelson Education, 2010.

Hofstede, Geert. *Culture's Consequences: Comparing Values, Behaviors, Institutions and Organizations Across Nations.* 2nd edition. Thousand Oaks, CA: Sage Publications, 2001.

Immigration to the United States <www.en.wikipedia.org/wiki/immigration_to_the_united_states>

Joshee, Reva and L. Johnson. *Multicultural Education Policies in Canada and the United States.* Vancouver, BC: UBC Press, 2008.

Levitan, Seymour, (ed). *I'm Not in My Homeland Anymore: Voices of Students in a New Land.* Toronto, ON: Pippin Publishing, 1998.

Linse, Caroline. "Language Issue or Learning Disability?" In *Essential Teacher*, Volume 5, issue 4, pp. 28-30. Alexandria, VA: TESOL Inc., December 2008.

Miner, Horace M. "Body Ritual among the Nacirema," in Luce, F. and E.C. Smith, eds. *Towards Internationalism: Readings in Cross-Cultural Communication*, pp. 241-246. Cambridge, MA: Newbury House/Harper and Row, 1987.

National Council of Teachers of English–Position Statements: *The NCTE Definition of 21st Century Literacies.* <www.ncte.org/positions/statements>

Ortiz, Alba. *English Language Learners with Special Needs: Effective Instructional Strategies.* 2001. <www.ldonline.org/article/5622>

Sasson, Dorit. "Building Fluency with Reluctant Junior High English Language Learners." In *Essential Teacher*, Vol. 5, issue 4 pp. 37-39. Alexandria, VA: TESOL Inc., December 2008.

Shearman, S. M. *Culture, Values and Cultural Variability: Reviews of Hofstede, Inglehart, and Schwartz Universal Frameworks.* Paper presented at the annual meeting of the International Communication Association, Montreal, QC. May 21, 2008. <www.allacademic.com/meta/p234591_index.html>

World Values Survey. (WVS 2005 Wave Data Files). <wvsevsdb.com/wvs/WVSData.jsp>

Spanish Language. Britannica Concise Encyclopedia. <www.answers.com/topic/spanish-language>

Refugees Worldwide.
<www.unhcr.org>

Yearbook of Immigration Statistics (published annually). <www.dhs.gov/files/statistics/publications/yearbook.shtm>

Learning More

Cary, Stephen. *Working with Second Language Learners: Answers to Teachers' Top Ten Questions.* 2nd. ed. Portsmouth, NH: Heinemann, 2007.

Coelho, Elizabeth. *Adding English: A Guide to Teaching in Multilingual Classrooms.* Toronto, ON: Pippin Publishing, 2004.

Cole, Robert W., (ed). *Educating Everybody's Children: Diverse Teaching Strategies for Diverse Learners,* 2nd. edition. Alexandria, VA: Association for Supervision and Curriculum Development (ASCD), 2008.

Critical Issue: Educating Teachers for Diversity
<www.ncrel.org/sdrs/areas/issues/educatrs/presrvce/pe300.htm>
North Central Regional Education Laboratory created this paper some years ago. It is still very relevant and worthwhile today.

Cummins, Jim. "Affirming Identity in Multilingual Classrooms" in *Educational Leadership*, Volume 63, number 1, pp 38-43, September 2005. <www.ascd.org/ASCD/pdf/journals/ed_lead/el200509_cummins.pdf>

Gunderson, Lee. *ESL (ELL) Literacy Instruction: A Guidebook to Theory and Practice.* 2nd. edition. New York, NY: Routledge, 2009.

Haynes, Judie and D. Zacarian. *Teaching English Language Learners Across the Content Areas.* Alexandria, VA: ASCD, 2010.

Law, Barbara and M. Eckes. *The More-Than-Just-Surviving Handbook: ESL for Every Classroom Teacher.* 2nd. ed. Winnipeg, MB: Peguis Publishers, 2000.

Law, Barbara and M. Eckes. *Assessment and ESL: An Alternative Approach.* 2nd. ed. Winnipeg, MB: Portage and Main Press, 2007.

Ontario Ministry of Education. *Many Roots, Many Voices: Supporting English Language Learners in Every Classroom.* (n.d.) <www.edu.gov.on.ca/eng/document/manyroots/>

Reiss, Jodi. *Teaching Content to English Language Learners: Strategies for Secondary School Success.* White Plains, NY: Pearson Education, 2005.

Richard-Amato, Patricia and M. Snow. *Academic Success for English Language Learners: Strategies for K-12 Mainstream Teachers.* White Plains, NY: Pearson Education, 2004.

WEBSITES

<www.everythingesl.net/lessons/>
This site, hosted by Judie Haynes, has advice and lots of lessons, particularly content-based ESL lesson plans for beginning through intermediate (linguistic) level students. It is also constantly updated and features short, succinct articles of relevance to current issues and topics related to EAL learners.

The website of the National Clearinghouse for English Language Acquisition and Language Instruction Education Programs provides many worthwhile links, including Online Library, In the Classroom, Language and Education, Databases, and so on. To help you decide where to go, try clicking on "What's New" to check out the most recent research.

<www.ascd.org/default.aspx>
Though the Association for Supervision and Curriculum Development deals with more than EAL, it has produced many very fine publications that are pertinent to our work with EAL learners in a multi-ethnic classroom setting.

<www.cal.org>
This site is home of the Center for Applied Linguistics and houses an index with much information for classroom teachers new to working with EAL learners. Find the document titled *What Elementary Teachers Need to Know About Language* at <www.cal.org/resources/digest/0006fillmore.html>

Several provinces in Canada have, or are in the process of creating, curriculum specifically for EAL learners. Two examples are the links for these documents for the Ministries of Education in Ontario and Alberta.
<www.edu.gov.on.ca/eng/document/esleldprograms/guide.pdf>
<education.alberta.ca/media/507659/eslkto9gi.pdf>

Culture and Communication

Denton, Paula. "The Power of Our Words." In *Educational Leadership,* Vol. 66, no.1: Alexandria, VA: ASCD, September 2008.

Flaitz, Jeffra, (ed). *Understanding Your International Students: An Educational, Cultural and Linguistic Guide.* Ann Arbor, MI: University of Michigan Press, 2003.

Flaitz, Jeffra. *Understanding your Refugee and Immigrant Students: An Educational, Cultural and Linguistic Guide.* Ann Arbor, MI: University of Michigan Press, 2006.

Hawley, Willis and S. Nieto. *Another Inconvenient Truth: Race and Ethnicity Matter,* In *Educational Leadership,* Vol, 68, no. 3, pages 66-71. Alexandria, VA: ASCD. November 2010.

Li, Guofang. *Culturally Contested Pedagogy: Battles of Literacy and Schooling between Mainstream Teachers and Asian Immigrant Parents.* Albany, NY: State University of New York Press. 2006.

Skolnick, Joan, N. Dulberg and T. Maestre. *Through Other Eyes: Developing Empathy and Multicultural Perspectives in the Social Studies.* Toronto, ON: Pippin Publishing, 2004.

Waxler-Morrison, Nancy, E. Richardson, J. Anderson and N.A. Chambers, (eds). *Cross-Cultural Caring: A Handbook for Health Professionals,* 2nd ed. Vancouver, BC: UBC Press, 2006.

WEBSITES

<www.cp-pc.ca/english/>
These country profiles offer a snapshot of key elements including education, food, communication, spirituality, work, family life, history, and so on. (Caution: these documents have not been updated since 2002)

<news.bbc.co.uk/2/hi/country_profiles/default.stm>
Full profiles provide an instant guide to the history, politics and economies of countries and territories, as well as background on key institutions. They also include audio and video clips from BBC archives.

<www.cia.gov/library/publications/the-world-factbook/index.html>
This site provides a great deal of information as the previous listing above, but in addition provides maps, flags and country comparisons.

<www.crosscultured.com/index.php>
CrossCultural Development Educational Services, a small company based in Washington State, provides presentations and workshops, as well as many useful products. Two of its notable publications are *Cognitive Learning Styles & Strategies for Diverse Learners* and *Separating Difference from Disability.* (Corwin Press

recently (2010) published *RTI for Diverse Learners,* authored by Dr. Catherine Collier, director of CCDES.)

<www.nafsa.org/publication.sec/epublications/online_guide_to/>
This site is hosted by NAFSA: Association of International Educators, and provides an on-line guide to educational systems around the world. This site is particularly useful when trying to evaluate course equivalencies and credits at the secondary level.

Working with Special Learners

English Language Learners with Learning Disabilities (Colorin Colorado)
<www.colorincolorado.org/webcasts/disabilities>

English Language Learners with Special Needs: Effective Instructional Strategies (CAL)
<www.cal.org/resources/digest/0108ortiz.html>

Hamayan, Else, B. Marler, C. Sanchez-Lopez and J. Damico. *Special Education Considerations for English Language Learners: Delivering a Continuum of Services.* Philadelphia, PA: Caslon Inc. 2007.

Harris, Carole R. "Identifying and Serving Recent Immigrant Children Who Are Gifted." ERIC DIGEST (EC E520) 1993.
<eric.hoagiesgifted.org/e520.html>

How Can Teachers Nurture Giftedness in Children Whose First Language Is Not English and Who Are Limited in English Proficiency? (ERIC EC) 2003.
<www.hoagiesgifted.org/eric/faq/gt-esl.html>

Teaching English-Language Learners with Learning Difficulties (TeacherVision)
< www.teachervision.fen.com/learning-disabilities/bilingual education/10267.html>

<www.brycs.org>
Bridging Refugee Youth & Children's Services is a vast resource for information about working with refugee learners from around the world. There are also many downloadable teaching and learning resources.

<www.ldonline.org>
LD OnLine is a huge database of information about children with additional learning challenges.

<www.hoagiesgifted.org>
Hoagies' Gifted Education Page focuses on gifted learners and their needs.

<www.crosscultured.com/index.php>
There are a number of downloadables that focus on supporting learners with additional challenges, but two notable (to purchase) publications are *Cognitive Learning Strategies for Diverse Learners* and *Separating Difference from Disability*. In addition, as noted in an earlier entry, Corwin Press recently (2010) published *RTI for Diverse Learners,* authored by Dr. Catherine Collier, director of CCDES.

Graphic Organizers are a boon to all learners, highly recommended for EAL learners, and particularly helpful for those learners with additional challenges. That is why a few starting points are listed for you here.

Instructional Strategies Online: What are Graphic Organizers? (Saskatoon Public Schools)
<olc.spsd.sk.ca/de/pd/instr/strats/graphicorganizers/index.html>

This collection of ready-to-use graphic organizers will help students classify ideas and communicate more effectively.
<www.graphic.org/goindex.html>

Graphic Organizers (Terri Sigueza, 2005)
<www.colorincolorado.org/article/13354>

Graphic Organizers for Content Instruction (Judie Haynes)
<www.everythingesl.net/inservices/graphic_organizers.
php>

Strategies, Resources and Materials

Brear. Donald, L. Helman, S. Templeton, M. Invernizzi and F. Johnston. *Words Their Way: Word Study for Phonics, Vocabulary and Spelling Instruction.* Upper Saddle River, NJ: Pearson Education, 2008.

Brownlie, Faye, Feniak C. and V. McCarthy. *Instruction and Assessment of ESL Learners: Promoting Success in Your Classroom.* Winnipeg, MB: Portage & Main Press, 2004.

Buehl, Doug. *Classroom Strategies for Interactive Learning.* 3rd. ed. Newark, DE: International Reading Association, Inc., 2009.

Clark, Raymond C., A. A. Burrows, Patrick R. Moran. *The ESL Miscellany: A Treasury of Cultural and Linguistic Information.* 3rd. ed. Brattleboro, VT: Pro Lingua Associates, 2000.

Reiss, Jodi. *Teaching Content to English Language Learners: Strategies for Secondary School Success.* White Plains, NY: Pearson Education, 2005.

Reiss, Jodi. *102 Content Strategies for English Language Learners: Teaching for Academic Success in Grades 3-12.* White Plains, NY: Pearson Education. 2007.

Robb, Laura. *Teaching Reading in Social Studies, Science, and Math: Practical Ways to Weave Comprehension Strategies into Your Content Area Teaching.* New York, NY: Scholastic, 2003.

Ruggiano Schmidt, Patricia and Wen Ma. *50 Literacy Strategies for Culturally Responsive Teaching, K-8.* Thousand Oaks, CA: Corwin Press, 2006.

As mentioned previously, Graphic Organizers are an invaluable resource for EAL learners. A few starting points are listed for you here.

> Instructional Strategies Online: What are Graphic Organizers? (Saskatoon Public Schools)
> <http://olc.spsd.sk.ca/de/pd/instr/strats/graphicorganiz ers/index.html>

> This collection of ready-to-use graphic organizers will help students classify ideas and communicate more effectively. <www.graphic.org/goindex.html>

> Graphic Organizers (Terri Sigueza, 2005)
> <www.colorincolorado.org/article/13354>

> Graphic Organizers for Content Instruction (Judie Haynes)
> <www.everythingesl.net/inservices/graphic_organizers. php>

Websites for Teachers and Learners

<www.eslgold.com>
ESLgold.com (ESL: English Study and Learning Materials) offers ESL materials across the grades. (Also offers a wide range of materials available in many other languages)

<www.eslcafe.com/idea/index.cgi>
Dave's ESL Café Idea Cookbook has been around for some time. There are currently 2101 recipes (ideas) in 26 categories in this cookbook. There is a wide range in terms of age suitability.

<www.english-at-home.com>
This site has quite a few resources for learning English, such as English speaking, English pronunciation, grammar and vocabulary.

<www.1-language.com/eslactivityzone/index.htm>
ESL Activities Zone has something for all levels—plenty of lesson plan ideas here!

\<www.1-language.com/eslflashcards/index.htm\>
There are many flashcards to choose from here, with 138 cards currently available.

\<mrshurleysesl.com\>
Links to a wide range of ESL sites. At the top of the page, click on "Teacher Resources" for a wide array of sample lessons and ideas.

\<www.teflgames.com\>
Have fun and improve your English by playing some of the free matching games online; opposites, synonyms, general phrases and more.

\<www.manythings.org\>
This is an enjoyable study site for older students of English as a Second Language.

\<www.eslconnect.com/links.html\>
Here are more than 200 sites with an abundance of ESL information for teachers and students.

\<www.internet4classrooms.com/esl.htm\>
This website is the repository of a large storehouse of useful links.

\<www.nelliemuller.com/ESL_WebQuests.htm\>
Dozens of webquests categorized by age groups and content topics.